Quick Callanetics

For Your Legs

Quick Callanetics

For Your Legs

Callan Pinckney

First Published in 1992 by Vermilion, an imprint of Ebury Publishing
Ebury Publishing is a Random House Group Company
Random House
20 Vauxhall Bridge Road
London SW1V 2SA

Pinckney, Callan
Quick callanetics - Legs: The shapeliest legs in only 20 minutes a day.
I. Title
613.7

ISBN 9780091954840

Edited by Emma Callery
Designed by Clive Dorman
Typeset in Times New Roman by Clive Dorman

Printed and bound in Great Britain by Clays Ltd, St Ives plc

WARNING:

There are risks inherent in any exercise programme. The advice of a doctor should be obtained prior to embarking on any exercise regimen. This programme is intended for persons in good health.

TO PREGNANT WOMEN:

Under no circumstances should any woman in the first trimester of their pregnancy do any of the exercises which also use the stomach muscles featured in this book. During the second and third trimester do not attempt to do the exercises unless your doctor has actually done them to feel how deep the contractions are.

Do not just show your doctor the book. These exercises appear to be very easy, but looks in this case are extremely deceiving.

CONTENTS

INTRODUCTION

Welcome to Quick Callanetics. Whether you regularly practise a Callanetics programme using a book, video, or an authorized class in one of our new studios, or you are experiencing Callanetics for the first time, this book will give you safe, fast and effective results if followed properly. By using the basic programme set out in the original book, millions of readers have already discovered that Callanetics is a safe and quick way to change bodyshape to give the firm, attractive body we all dream about. Those mastering that programme have graduated to *Super Callanetics*. *Callanetics Countdown* presents a shorter programme for those with more demanding time schedules and if you are seeking a more gradual introduction to the basic Callanetics one-hour programme. *Callanetics for Your Back* is for those people with backaches or back problems. The book is designed to correct the problem or to make the back more flexible and to release pain. The exercises are also preventative for those who don't have back problems and never want to have them as the stretches and contractions actually strengthen the back. The appeal has proven to be international, with books now published in many countries around the world.

The huge success of the first Callanetics book brought a demand for videos; which include the original *Callanetics: Ten Years Younger in Ten Hours*, followed by *Beginning Callanetics* and *Super Callanetics*. Now we have the new *Quick Callanetics* series with three 20-minute workout tapes for the legs, stomach, and hips and behind. This book contains all the exercises, and more, as featured in *Quick Callanetics: Legs.*

We all share common problems and have as our goal a strong, firm and shapely body, but our bodies also differ in various ways. A person may have a special problem in one area and much less of a problem elsewhere. Some of us have special problems with our legs or thighs, or both. The inner thighs are especially hard to firm up. Often the front thigh firms up leaving the inner thigh looking even more flabby and wobbly than ever. That is because many exercises for this part of the body are incomplete. But in Quick Callanetics you will find the all-important inner-thigh squeeze which supplies the contraction to complete the process of firming up the legs.

Through a series of stretching and contracting exercises the Quick Callanetics programme is designed to give you those long, tight legs we all admire. At the same, the knees, hips and ankles are protected against injury. However, I must caution anyone who has had knee problems to consult their doctor before attempting these exercises. So, do what you can but do not force your legs to stretch more than they are capable. Your muscles will stretch beautifully when they are ready, not when you command them. This can cause injuries. Don't force the leg higher than it can reach and never jerk the body. Don't worry if you cling to the barre or furniture for dear life at first. As you become stronger, your need for support will lessen. These are slow, gentle stretches that lengthen the muscles avoiding bulk and front thigh bulge for a shapely, firm, long look.

As you work on your legs and thighs, you are working for the perfect legs - the look that allows a coin to be placed and held by the four places a woman's legs should touch - the inner thighs, knees, calves and ankles. It is a look most of us can achieve.

THE ORIGINS OF CALLANETICS

I grew up in the deep South of the United Sates, Georgia to be exact, born of a long line of Pinckneys whose ancestors include the first Viscount of Surrey. They fought with William the Conqueror in the Norman Invasion in 1066. I found a life of well-bred tradition restricting, but not so the Pinckney fighting spirit. And I had to fight from the beginning for I was born with curvature of the spine caused by scoliosis and I had to wear steel leg braces for seven years to correct my club feet. It was only twelve years of ballet classes which helped to turn my feet outward.

After two years of college I decided to explore the world, going first to Europe and then setting off to explore Africa, Asia and finally the Far East. I worked hard doing manual labour to make ends meet, and I further damaged my already abused body by carrying a backpack that almost equalled my weight, doing much of my travelling by foot. At 5' 1", I had always been petite. The starchy foods, such as digestive biscuits, and 40 cups of heavily sugared tea a day in England pushed my weight up to 129lb (9st 3lb). I developed a middle-age spread. Later my weight dropped to 78lb (5st 8lb) as a result of amoebic dysentery contracted during my travels. I lost muscle tone. I strained my back and knees, and my behind sagged and spread, making my outer thighs look like saddlebags.

Returning to the United States after eleven years, my physical condition was desperate. I had been told earlier by doctors that if I didn't have immediate surgery on my back and knees I could spend the rest of my life in a wheelchair. I could not allow this to happen, but I was unwilling to face the possibility of scarring from surgery. Within a year I could barely get out of bed.

Developing Callanetics

In the exercise classes I started attending on my return to the States I was shocked that most of them put a strain on the back. The movements were impossible for me, so I began to develop exercises to accommodate my physical condition. During my travels I had experienced a great number of exercise techniques, including belly dancing in the Middle East, and I remembered my earlier ballet training. Gradually I evolved a slow, gentle way to position my body into movements which protected the back. Instead of applying pressure to the lower back, I developed exercises which stretched the spine. At the same time, they penetrated deep into the body to reach muscles and shape and tone them with amazing speed. I learnt that the circular motions used in belly dancing loosened the pelvic area, gradually allowing movements in the sacrum area (lower back) where I had no flexibility left.

Each motion was delicate and precise, involving ¼ to ½ inch – tiny movements were all my body was capable of doing at the time. But these tiny motions focused the muscles in a remarkable way. In addition to correcting my physical problems, I noticed my behind pulling up and in, my stomach flattening, my posture improving dramatically day by day, my thighs becoming firm and youthful along with my inner thighs and underarms. I no longer wobbled when I walked and my arms did not jiggle when I waved. I felt totally comfortable in shorts or a sleeveless dress. My body was becoming incredibly strong and felt years younger. Friends noticed the change in my body. They wanted to know my secret. I showed them my exercises, and they also got the same, safe, quick results.

The First Callanetics Book

For the next eleven years I taught small classes of students who had heard about my exercises from their friends. My students had noticed remarkable changes in their bodies. For lack of a name for my exercises, my students named them 'Callanetics', and they also said it made their bodies feel 'ten years younger in ten hours'. They encouraged me to write a book. Finally, I called an agent. The book was a hard one to sell, I was told. I was not a celebrity, model or movie star. And it seemed that at the time every celebrity, model and movie star in the world had an exercise book on the market. Furthermore, I was not aerobic and aerobics were in vogue. But the agent was convinced by my exercises, just as my students had been, and the book was eventually sold to a publisher for a very modest advance.

Then came the crushing news. Of the few thousand books printed and distributed, over half had been returned unsold. I was too unknown. The publisher was to abandon the book and sell the remaining copies at cost. However, I knew that if I could only reach the public, they would recognize the value of my programme and reap the benefits of Callanetics just as my students had done. I did everything I could think of to bring the book to the attention of the public. When I went to Chicago for a final television appearance, magic happened and 14 months of hard work promoting the book paid off. As a result of that single television appearance, enough copies were sold in a week to place the book on *The New York Times* bestseller list in the number two position. It remained on the list for almost a year. That success has now been repeated in many other countries including Britain. I will be forever grateful to all those people who brought Callanetics to the attention of the public. And I am grateful to all of you who told your friends of the great results achieved through Callanetics.

CALLANETICS TODAY

Today, those of you who practise Callanetics are legion with more continuously joining the ranks. As this is being written, the word 'Callanetics' is entering the language through the *Collins English Dictionary* which defines Callanetics as 'a system of exercise involving repetition of small muscular movements and contractions, designed to improve muscle tone.' And what brought all this about? The answer is simple: RESULTS. The programme works for anyone of any age giving the fastest results in the shortest time with no injuries.

When I launched the original Callanetics programme, I introduced myself as a teacher. At the time the video was released I was 47 years old. Well, time marches on and I am now 52, and I am still a teacher. Now I teach Master Teachers who teach others. Callanetics has grown enormously from the days when I taught small, private classes in my small studio on New York's mid-East Side.

In November 1990, another major chapter in the story of Callanetics started with the opening of the Callanetics Franchise Corporation with headquarters in Denver, Colorado. Since the introduction of the books and videos, I was deluged with requests for classes and qualified Callanetics teachers. It became obvious that a programme for training and certifying instructors to teach Callanetics was needed. This was especially so in light of reports that classes were being offered by unauthorized persons with no assurance that the exercises were being taught safely or effectively. Now, however, you can receive qualified instruction throughout the United States and several other countries including Great Britain, Belgium, Mexico and Australia, with teachers who have been properly trained and are certified. You will find further information on how to find classes or how to open your own studio at the beginning of this book. I urge you to seek instruction only from those studios who document their certification and are listed by the Callanetics Franchise Corporation.

Adverse Reactions

I am very annoyed when Callanetics is attacked by those who have not tried the programme and cannot speak first hand of its safety and benefits. The same is true of other so-called exercise experts who feel it necessary to protect their interests by being critical of Callanetics. Rather than pointing out what other programmes can't and don't do and the injury they can cause, I have always maintained the positive value that my programmes can give. I have always said, 'My only competition is plastic surgery', and that is still true.

Using Quick Callanetics

You may use this book in several ways. It is small and compact and can travel with you from home to work, on business trips or vacations, or wherever you choose to give yourself a quick reminder of the steps of the programme. If you are taking Callanetics classes in an authorized studio, you can use this book as a brush up source between classes. If you use an audio or video tape, this book will freeze the motion with a written explanation of how the movements work and will help you fix the precision of the position.

The book is divided into easy-to-follow sections. First there is the Quick Callanetics programme, exactly following the routine on the video. Should you find the Quick Callanetics programme too difficult at first, the Build Your Strength section will soon enable you to work through the exercises with ease. Please note that some of the photographs in the book show you the ultimate goal of Callanetics. Do not worry if you can't do the same immediately – always work at your own pace.

Triple slow motion

The movements in Callanetics are tiny, delicate, gentle, and precise. They are done very slowly, as I have always said 'in triple slow motion'. Think of Callanetics as meditation in motion. In this way you reach deep, deep into the body to work the large muscles, as though working through them layer by layer. Never jerk and never bounce. Know how tiny ¼ to ½ of an inch is. Measure it! The movement is a pulse. If the directions call for 25 repetitions, think of it as 25 pulses. Do that amount of movement slowly and gently. Only when you are aware of the smallness and the gentleness of the movements, are you ready to d o Callanetics correctly. You will then find your muscles will perform at the level they are best able to. Don't be upset if you have to take frequent breaks or if you can only do a few repetitions at first. You will be surprised at how much stronger you will become in very little time.

No forcing

Because it is so important, let me emphasise that you must not force. If you are stretching, your muscles will only stretch at their capacity and you should not force them beyond that level. While you are contracting, or strengthening the muscles, you should not be able to do more repetitions than the muscles will allow at that particular time. This prevents you from forcing the muscles beyond their limitations. Forcing the muscles can result in exhaustion or injury.

Do not – I repeat – do not be distressed or disappointed if you can only do two or three repetitions at the beginning, this is a natural process. With each session you will become stronger, and you will be able to do more. The most important goal is to learn to protect and respect your back to prevent back pain and to relieve back problems.

Curling up the pelvis

If there is one motion that is the key to Callanetics, it is curling up the pelvis, the link between the upper and lower body. Tighten your buttocks, and in triple slow motion try to move, or 'curl up', the pelvic area, as if you were trying to bring your pubic bone to your naval. Imagine there is a string attached to the bottom of your leotard. Gently pull straight up on the string and your pelvis will curl up. This movement stretches your spine, and strengthens your abdominal, inner- and front-thigh, and buttock muscles, as well as your calves and feet, if you are standing. Gaining freedom in the pelvic area is very important because it affects posture, balance, and alignment of the body. It also loosens the hip joints and allows for more fluid movements. The more the pelvis is curled up, the deeper the buttock muscles contract and the faster the results.

Breathing

Always try to breathe naturally - and remember to breathe! Many people actually forget to breathe when exercising.

Counting

Several of the exercises include instructions to 'hold for a count of ...' You should count 'one thousand and one, one thousand and two,' etc. If you count aloud, the added plus is that you will be sure to breathe!

Think relaxation

Don't tense the body. Let the gentleness control the motion. By not forcing you will gain the full benefits of an exercise without exhausting the muscles or yourself. Exert the minimum amount of effort for maximum results. This is not to say you will not feel the exercises. You will feel them working deep in specific areas, without straining other parts of the body, particularly the back.

Commitment

Think, 'This is my time – a time I give to myself.' Think beautiful, soft thoughts; allow yourself to visualize and fantasize. You have done more than enough for everyone else. Now it is your turn. You will eventually attach the same importance to yourself as you do to the other elements of your life. Because it is fast and effective, Callanetics will fit into any schedule and can be done anywhere as it does not require special equipment. Just 20 minutes a day will produce results you will be extremely proud of. The other books in the series deal with the hips and behind, and the stomach.

This programme is designed just for you. So let's get started. You'll be surprised how quickly you will see results and be capable of doing the required repetitions with ease. And remember, *gentleness* is the key word.

QUICK CALLANETICS

THE FOLLOWING EXERCISES:

• MAKE THE LEGS TIGHTER AND LONGER LOOKING •

• ELIMINATE SAGGING KNEES •

• TIGHTEN GOOSHY, SAGGING SKIN •

• CREATE BEAUTIFUL SHAPELY LEGS •

REMEMBER: All the pictures show the ultimate position which may be achieved. Don't expect to attain these positions immediately. With patience and time, you will be amazed at how much you are capable of stretching and strengthening, and your body will love you for it.

Do not force your stretch. You must respect the level you are capable of. Injuries can occur when the stretch is forced. The muscle will stretch when it is ready to, not when you command it to.

Most people will start by putting their foot or heel on a footstool, or seat of a chair and work up from there. The more your hamstrings are stretched the more you can lift your leg.

PLEASE NOTE: This series of exercises may appear complicated at first. Please be sure to read through the text to get an understanding of what you must do before attempting them. The benefits will be well worth it. Don't worry about doing these exercises at exactly the level shown in the photographs. Do them at your own level, which is perfect for you. If you can only do five pulses at first, that is your level. As your muscles strengthen, your form will improve. Don't be discouraged, you will be able to do more repetitions each time you do the exercises. You'll be working the muscles deeper and deeper, and in no time at all each exercise will be a breeze. It is advisable not to wear shoes for any of these exercises; the weight of them is simply too heavy.

If you have knee problems, do the exercises very gently and slowly. They should not aggravate any existing problems. In fact, many students with knee problems due to injuries, arthritis, or even surgery have reported that these exercises improved their conditions tremendously. Just be cautious and use your judgment. You'll find that practising these exercises can actually help decrease the likelihood of future injuries in any activity by strengthening your leg muscles. Since these muscles are the same ones that assist the back muscles in everyday activities, the extra bonus is that you will be less likely to have any problems running, walking or standing.

REMEMBER:

• NO BOUNCING •

• NO JERKING •

• NO FORCING •

• WORK AT YOUR OWN PACE •

• ALWAYS TAKE BREATHERS IF NECESSARY •

• GENTLENESS IS THE KEY TO THESE EXERCISES •

Up and Down

THIS EXERCISE:

• STRETCHES THE SPINE •

• LOOSENS THE KNEES •

TECHNIQUE

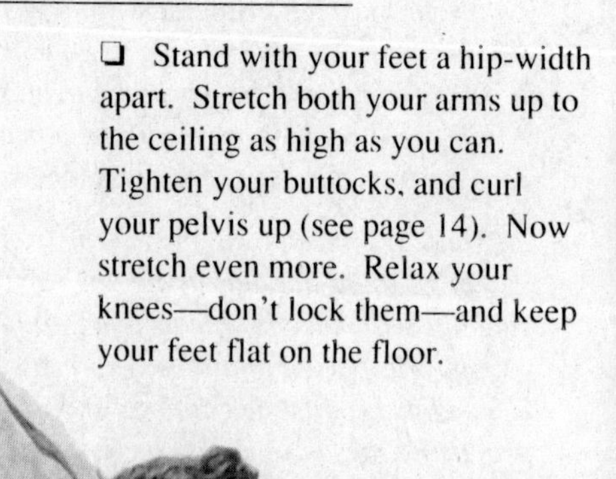

❑ Stand with your feet a hip-width apart. Stretch both your arms up to the ceiling as high as you can. Tighten your buttocks, and curl your pelvis up (see page 14). Now stretch even more. Relax your knees—don't lock them—and keep your feet flat on the floor.

❑ In one smooth motion, gently bend your knees as much as you can, and lower your upper body towards the floor, with your arms reaching forward. Imagine you are trying to grasp an object on the floor in front of you. Your torso is stretching out and away.

❑ Gently swing your arms back, raising them as high as you can behind your body. Your knees will straighten slightly and your buttocks will raise with the motion of your arms going to the back and then up.

NOTE: When you have swung your arms back, as above, this will be one of the few instances where your pelvis will not be curled up.

❑ Just as you are about to reverse the motion to go back up to your starting position, tighten your buttocks and curl your pelvis up even more than you think you can. Keep it curled up until you return, arms once again stretching up towards the ceiling. If you have a swayback, tip your pelvis up as much as you can.

Repetitions

WORK UP TO 5

DON'TS

❑ Do not arch your back while stretching your arms up to the ceiling.

❑ Do not tense your knees or feet.

❑ Do not tense your shoulders or neck.

The Neck Relaxer

THIS EXERCISE:

• LOOSENS THE NECK AND SHOULDERS •

• STRETCHES THE SPINE •

• INCREASES JOINT FLEXIBILITY •

• RELEASES TENSION IN THE NECK AND BETWEEN THE SHOULDER BLADES •

TECHNIQUE

❑ Stand erect, feet a hip-width apart. Relax your shoulders and bend your knees. Tighten your buttocks, and curl your pelvis up more than you think you can.

❑ In triple slow motion, roll your head down, resting your chin on your chest.

❑ Still slowly, move your chin over to your right shoulder as far as you can.

❑ Then aim your chin up towards the ceiling as high as you can, at the same time stretching the back of your neck up.

❑ Delicately bring your chin back down to your chest.

❑ Gently move your chin over your left shoulder, and then stretch it up as high as it will go.

❑ Bring it back down to where your chin touches your chest again. This is one repetition.

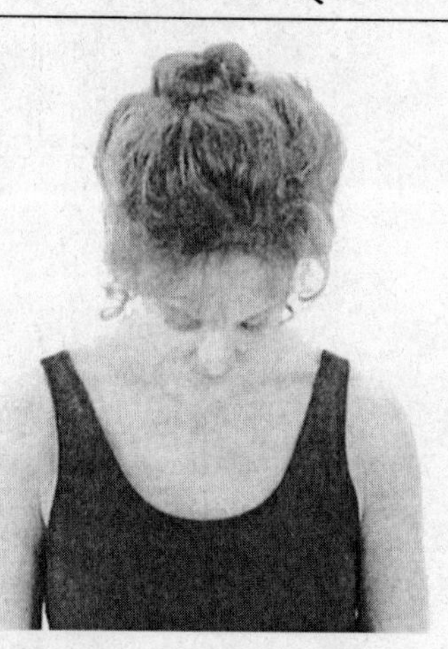

Repetitions TO EACH SIDE
5

DON'TS
❑ Do not make any harsh or sudden movements.
❑ Do not hunch or tense your shoulders.
❑ Do not tense your jaw.
❑ Do not lock your knees.
❑ Do not stick out your stomach or arch your lower back.

The Pelvic Wave

THIS EXERCISE:

• STRENGTHENS AND TIGHTENS THE LEGS, THE BUTTOCKS, AND THE ABDOMINAL MUSCLES •

• STRETCHES THE SPINE AND THE AREA BETWEEN THE SHOULDER BLADES •

• KEEPS THE PELVIS FLEXIBLE •

• WORKS THE FRONT AND INNER THIGHS, FEET, ANKLES, AND CALVES •

NOTE: The barre used in the following exercises could be made from almost any piece of sturdy furniture such as a sofa or chair. Choose a height that is comfortable for you.

TECHNIQUE

❑ Stand at your barre, or hold onto a sturdy piece of furniture, go up on the balls of your feet, heels together, knees bent, and arms straight, but relaxed.

❑ Keep your back straight and relaxed (if possible), and do not force the knees out to the sides at all.

- In triple slow motion, with your torso erect and your neck stretched towards the ceiling, lower your torso 1 inch straight down towards the floor.

- Tighten your buttocks and curl your pelvis up. Then curl it up even more than you think you can, and at the same time allow your upper torso to round as much as possible. Gently release your pelvis without pushing your buttocks back.

- In triple slow motion, go down 1 more inch, tighten your buttocks, curl your pelvis up even more, and gently release.

- Go down another 1 inch, tighten your buttocks, curl your pelvis up even more, and gently release.

- Feel how much your inner thighs are working at this level.

❑ Now reverse the movement, going up 1 inch each time, just as slowly, until you have returned to the original standing position. This equals 1 repetition.

Repetitions
WORK UP TO 5

DON'TS

❑ **Do not forget that for the second and third sets, you should curl your pelvis up even more each time.**
❑ **Do not stick out your buttocks when coming out of the pelvic curl. Your spine is always straight when your pelvis is not curled up.**
❑ **Do not arch your back.**
❑ **Do not try to aim your knees out too far to the side. Let their position be natural.**
❑ **Do not tense your shoulders. Your upper back should be as round as possible when curling up the pelvis for the most beneficial spine stretch. The more your pelvis is curled up, the more your torso will round, stretching the spine, and the faster your legs will become strong and tight.**
❑ **Do not lean your weight on the barre. Keep your balance on the balls of your feet.**
❑ **Do not allow your buttocks to go below your knees when lowering your torso. This puts too much pressure on your knees.**
❑ **Do not let your buttocks rest above or in front of your heels. The buttocks should be behind your heels.**

Plié and Balance

THIS EXERCISE:

• STRENGTHENS AND TIGHTENS THE LEG MUSCLES, ESPECIALLY THOSE OF THE FRONT AND INNER THIGHS •

TECHNIQUE

❑ Beginning in the same position as The Pelvic Wave, hold your barre or piece of sturdy furniture with both hands, your arms straight and loose, and stand on the balls of your feet with your heels together.

❑ In triple slow motion, lower your torso straight down, 1 inch.

❑ In triple slow motion, raise yourself back up, breathing normally. This exercise is done in one smooth motion.

❑ The slower you do this exercise, the stronger your front thigh muscles will become. Also, the more erect your torso, the more your thigh muscles are worked.

❑ As you become stronger you will be able to take your torso down further, but never let your buttocks go lower than your knees.

NOTE: At first your torso may be rounded towards the barre and you will be holding on to the barre for dear life. As you become stronger, you will eventually be able to hold your torso perfectly erect, and your hands will just be resting on the barre.

Repetitions

WORK UP TO 10

IF YOU WANT A MORE INTENSE EXERCISE:

Hold your lowered position for a slow count of 3 to 5 before coming back up.

DON'TS

- ❑ **Do not let your heels drop to the floor when coming up.**
- ❑ **Do not allow your buttocks to go below your knees when lowering your torso. This would mean putting too much pressure on your knees.**
- ❑ **Do not tense your shoulders.**
- ❑ **Do not arch your back or stick out your buttocks. Keep your spine straight and your neck stretched.**

REMEMBER:

Always take a breather if you feel the exercise is getting too difficult. In a few sessions, this exercise will become increasingly easy.

The Hamstring Stretch (Up and Over)

While doing this hamstring stretch, most people take the foot they're standing on directly out to the side (usually for balance). Try to learn to aim the foot forward (train yourself to do this).

THIS EXERCISE:

• STRETCHES THE NECK, SPINE, BETWEEN THE SHOULDER BLADES, THE BUTTOCKS, THE INNER THIGHS, THE HAMSTRING MUSCLES, AND THE CALVES •

NOTE: If you have sciatica, always keep your knees bent during this exercise, to relieve pressure on your lower back.

TECHNIQUE

NOTE: You will start much lower, perhaps even bending the knee of the raised leg. Many people eventually achieve the position of the leg shown here. Find out what your limitations are by gently trying different positions and heights before you begin. At first, your head and torso may not move at all towards the legs. In a short time you will have much more flexibility.

❑ Standing straight, take your right leg up and rest your heel on your barre or piece of furniture. Your left foot should be turned out slightly for balance, with your left knee straight but relaxed.

❑ Stretch your torso and arms up towards the ceiling. Turn to the side, stretch up even more and then turn back to the front. Still stretching up, slowly round your torso over your right leg.

❑ When you're over as far as you can go, gently criss-cross your hands on your shin or front thigh (not the knee), letting them rest lightly. Take your elbows out to the side. Do not lock your knees.

❑ Gently move your torso up and down ¼ to ½ inch, or just hold the position.

❑ To come out of this exercise, slowly round your torso up, and gently take your right leg to the floor in triple slow motion.

❑ Repeat this exercise on the opposite side.

REMEMBER: A lot of people, especially women, have knees that bulge quite a bit on the inside of their legs. To make this area thinner and smoother, gently turn your raised leg and foot out to the side slightly—your right leg to the right or your left leg to the left.

Repetitions
TO EACH SIDE

WORK UP TO 50

DON'TS

❑ Do not be uncomfortable when doing this exercise. If resting your heel on your barre or piece of furniture is uncomfortable, place a facecloth under your ankle.

❑ Do not turn the foot you're standing on directly out to the side—unless that is the only way you can keep your balance—and keep that knee relaxed.

❑ Do not allow your hips to become uneven.

❑ Do not straighten your elbows. Keep them bent and stretched out.

❑ Do not rest your hands on your knees.

❑ Do not force your stretch.

❑ Do not lock your knees.

❑ Do not bounce.

IF YOU WANT MORE OF A STRETCH:

Once you're in position, try to put your head in between the left side of your right leg and crook of your arm. This is a lovely stretch for your neck and spine.

If that's too difficult or you're not quite stretched enough, you can move your hands up a little bit higher on your right leg, and rest your forehead on your leg, wherever it's comfortable (except directly on your kneecap). Or, gently take your standing leg back, away from the barre.

Open and Close

This exercise builds up incredible strength throughout the entire body. In ballet school, before classes, some students and I would do Open and Close for stamina, leg strength, and for a higher extension of the leg. At the beginning, the more you do, the lower your legs will go. Expect this—don't think you're not doing this exercise correctly if it happens! Believe it or not, there are some people in their seventies who can do fifty Open and Closes effortlessly, without breathers, and their legs remain at the same height.

As with so much of Callanetics, this is an exercise that must be respected. Most people with back problems have found that Open and Close has helped their backs tremendously—because they knew their own limitations and did not force the exercise. This means they stopped when they felt that the lower back was about to take over, and only did what they felt they could do properly at that particular time. Even though this is basically a leg exercise, it requires tremendous use of the stomach muscles as well. This is why, if your abdominals are not particularly strong, your lower back will inevitably take over—which is not what you want! Build yourself up slowly, and you'll soon find that another wonderful benefit of this exercise is that your stomach muscles also become stronger.

NOTE: If you feel you're losing strength, or your lower back is about to take over, lower your legs a few inches, or bend your knees as you open and close. Or take a breather. If you find that you're still feeling pressure on your lower back, you must discontinue this exercise until you have built up more strength in your stomach and leg muscles.

REMEMBER:

Height does not matter. Work at your own level. You may well find that to begin with you will simply be moving your legs across the floor. The photographs here indicate what can be achieved if you keep on working at Callanetics

BUT DON'T FORGET:

Open and Close must be treated with the respect it deserves!

NOTE: This is a wonderful exercise to do at the side of a desk or sofa to re-energise yourself during the day.

- ❑ You should be totally relaxed when starting this exercise. Sit on the floor with your upper back against a sofa or counter, and hold onto it as if there is a barre above your head. (Some people use a sturdy chest of drawers with one drawer open in place of a barre.) If you have a barre, sit under it with your hands or wrists draped lightly atop it. In the beginning, you will be hanging on for dear life.

- ❑ Bend your knees and take them up towards your chest. Point your toes. Scoot your buttocks forwards 4 to 5 inches so that you are not sitting on your tailbone. Gently drop your chin. This will help stretch your spine more.

❑ Slowly straighten your legs (although if you have sciatica, keep your knees bent), without locking your knees, pointing your toes up towards the ceiling as high as you can without forcing. You are sitting in a jack-knife position.

❑ In triple slow motion, open your legs as wide as you can, and then close them.

NOTE: It takes incredible strength for your legs to go this high with ease. Work at your own pace. Do not feel you should be achieving the same height immediately. You will be very surprised that by doing this exercise regularly you will quickly be able to achieve this height.

Repetitions
WORK UP TO 2 SETS OF 5

❑ To come out of this exercise, gently bend your knees in the closed position, bringing your legs in close to your body, and lower them to the floor.

WHEN THIS EXERCISE BECOMES TOO EASY:

Move your buttocks closer to the wall or piece of furniture, the more difficult this exercise. It is much harder to raise your legs when you are sitting that way just try one and you'll understand. The higher you can raise your legs, the more challenging Open and Close becomes.

DON'TS

❑ **Do not be in a position where you have to worry about the object you are holding on to being strong enough. Always make sure it is sturdy enough to hold your weight before you begin. Until you become stronger you will be holding on for dear life.**

❑ **Do not over do it. If your muscles are not particularly strong, stop and take breathers, and gradually work up to a set of 10, increasing slowly as your muscles tighten and strengthen.**

❑ **Do not allow yourself to become breathless. Take as many breathers as you wish.**

❑ **Do not tense your legs, especially the knees; eventually they will be as light as feathers.**

❑ **Do not move your chin up.**

❑ **Do not tense your feet but keep your toes pointed.**

❑ **Do not force your legs to move more than they can.**

The Hamstring and Calf Stretch

If you have sciatica, always keep your knees bent during this exercise, to relieve pressure on your back.

THIS EXERCISE:

• STRETCHES THE NECK, SPINE, BETWEEN THE SHOULDER BLADES, THE INNER THIGHS, AND THE BACKS OF THE LEGS, ESPECIALLY THE HAMSTRINGS •

• STRENGTHENS THE PECTORAL MUSCLES •

❑ Lie on your back, your feet a hip-width apart and bend your knees. Keep your feet flat on the floor. Try to flatten the back of your kneck on the floor.

❑ Bend your right knee up into your chest, and then gently straighten that leg as much as you can without forcing.

❑ Clasp your hands behind your right leg wherever it is comfortable (but not behind your knee). Take your elbows out and up, and in triple slow motion, bring your leg as close to your body as you can. At first, you may not be able to straighten your leg – this is natural. Work at your own pace.

❑ Gently straighten your left leg on the floor, without locking your knee, and rest your left heel on the floor.

❑ With an almost imperceptible motion, move your right leg towards your body, pulsing for ¼ to ½ inch. Always keep your elbows out.

NOTE: Gentleness with this stretch is the key word. This photograph shows your ultimate goal with this exercise.

FOR MORE OF A STRETCH, OR TO STRETCH YOUR CALVES:

Flex your feet towards you. Do not point them up towards the ceiling.

- ❑ To come out of this stretch, bend both your knees in a smooth, gentle motion, and place your feet flat on the floor. Bring your arms down as well, and rest them by your side.
- ❑ Repeat this exercise on the opposite side.

Repetitions TO EACH SIDE
WORK UP TO 50

DON'TS

- ❑ **Do not force your leg up higher than it can go.**
- ❑ **Do not lock your knees.**
- ❑ **Do not lift your resting leg from the floor. Keep it as straight and as low as possible, as long as your knee remains relaxed.**
- ❑ **Do not tense your raised leg. Keep the foot pointed but relaxed.**
- ❑ **Do not tighten your grasp on your leg.**
- ❑ **Do not tense your neck and shoulders. Take advantage of this time to relax your neck and entire body.**

The Inner-Thigh Stretch (Sitting)

THIS EXERCISE:

• STRETCHES THE INNER THIGHS, SPINE, NECK, UNDERARMS AND LEGS •

NOTE: Keep your torso relaxed. Never force your legs further than they can go. If you have sciatic pain, always keep your knees bent during this exercise. This will help relieve the pressure. If that is not helpful, discontinue this stretch until it is better.

Technique

❑ Sitting on the floor, stretch your legs out so they are spread as far apart as they can be without forcing. Place your hands either in front or behind you—whichever you prefer—and gently push your pelvis into the floor and scoot it forward a wee bit.

❑ Stretch your torso up, place your hands on your thighs, or in front of you on the floor. Take your elbows out, and round your upper back. Relax your shoulders and neck.

❑ Gently, round your upper back forward until your head and shoulders are down as far as they can go without forcing.

❑ Relax your body, and feel the stretch in your lower back and inner thighs. Stretch only as far as you are comfortable.

❑ Gently move your torso ¼ to ½ inch, up and down.

❑ As you become more stretched your torso will get closer to the floor. Always relax.

❑ When you have completed your repetitions slowly walk back up with your hands.

Repetitions
WORK UP TO **50**

❑ For more of a stretch, before you take your torso to the floor, clasp your hands behind you as high as you can. Then lower your toso to the floor. (If you are very stretched, you should be able to touch the floor with either your face, your nose, or your upper torso.)

DON'TS

❑ Do not force your body down.

❑ Do not bounce.

❑ Do not pull forward with your neck.

❑ Do not tense your legs. Relax your toes.

The Pelvic Rotation

NOTE: If you have knee problems, you can do the Pelvic Rotation in a standing position, with your knees bent. You will not see results as quickly, but as you already know, your health and safety are far more important! In the next two exercises most people with knee problems have experienced wonderful results.

THIS EXERCISE:

• STRENGTHENS THE BUTTOCKS, THIGHS, INNER THIGHS, LOWER BACK, STOMACH, AND PELVIC MUSCLES •

• STRETCHES THE ARMS AND SPINE •

• LOOSENS THE PELVIC AREA •

Technique

❑ On a mat, sit comfortably on your heels. Your knees are together and your legs relaxed.

❑ Stretch your arms up over your head and clasp your hands together. Keep your torso erect, and feel the stretch in your back.

❑ Lift your torso 3 inches up off your heels. If you find resting in this position difficult, lift your torso further up until you are comfortable.

❑ If you feel pressure on your calves, lean your torso forward as much as is necessary to release them. See photograph on page 41.

NOTE: The entire routine is one continuous slow motion.

❑ Take your right hip over to the right side as far as you can. Roll your pelvis forward, to the front, at the same time curling it up and aiming it into your navel. Move your left hip over to the left side as far as you can. Then move your buttocks to the back, completing a circle.

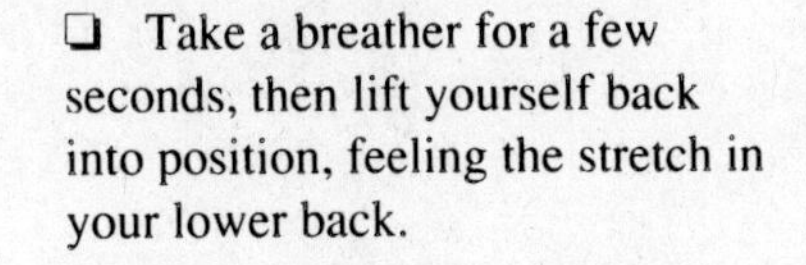

❑ Take a breather for a few seconds, then lift yourself back into position, feeling the stretch in your lower back.

❑ Repeat the Pelvic Rotation, starting to the left.

❑ Most men find it difficult to sit directly on the bottom of their feet. They can either turn both ankles out towards the floor—this creates a nice little hollow space for their buttocks to rest in. Or they can place the bottom of their toes on the floor and sit on their heels, which would then be facing up towards the ceiling.

Repetitions IN EACH DIRECTION
WORK UP TO 5

The motion is a smooth, flowing circle—hip—pelvis—hip—behind. Only your pelvis moves in an unbroken circle.

NOTE: At first, some people may experience some discomfort in their knees. Continue to do the exercises very gently but with your knees slightly apart. Soon the discomfort will subside, unless you have a medical problem.

DON'TS

- ❑ **Do not tense your body.**
- ❑ **Do not forget about your pelvis. The more you can curl it up into your navel when you rotate to the front, the more effective this exercise.**
- ❑ **Do not prevent yourself from taking breathers whenever you feel it necessary.**

The Pelvic Scoop

THIS EXERCISE:

• STRENGTHENS THE LEG MUSCLES, ESPECIALLY THE FRONT AND INNER-THIGH MUSCLES, THE STOMACH, BUTTOCKS, AND CALVES •

• STRETCHES THE SPINE•

TECHNIQUE

❏ Kneel on a mat, knees together, with your feet outstretched behind you and your legs relaxed. Keep your arms and shoulders relaxed and your spine straight.

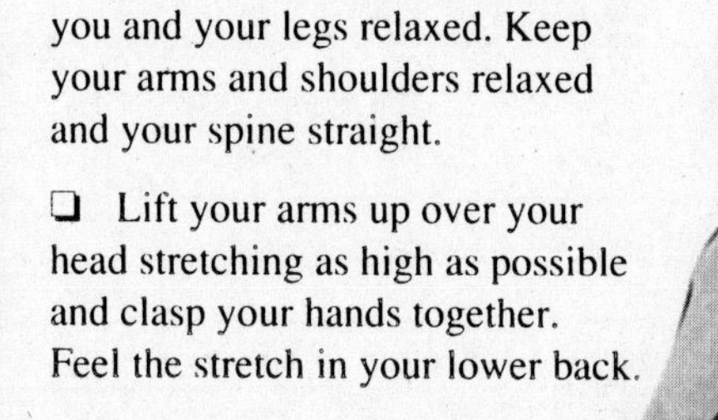

❏ Lift your arms up over your head stretching as high as possible and clasp your hands together. Feel the stretch in your lower back.

❏ Lower your arms in front about a foot. Round your torso a wee bit forward. Now, keeping your spine straight, aim your buttocks down towards your heels. Do not arch your back.

IF THIS EXERCISE IS TOO DIFFICULT:

Only lower your torso towards your heels as much as is comfortable. Do not feel you have to go all the way down.

❑ When you have stretched your buttocks to the point where they are delicately brushing your heels, gently tighten your buttocks, then curl your pelvis up even more than you think you can, in a slow scooping motion.

❑ Raise your arms back up till your hands are above your head in the starting position.

❑ Keep curling your pelvis up until you have returned to the original kneeling position. When your pelvis is curled up, your buttocks will be closer to your heels.

Repetitions
WORK UP TO **10**

NOTE: The stronger you are, the more you will be able to take your arms towards the back when you are scooping back up. Also, the more you can take your arms and torso back when you are returning to the original kneeling position with your curl-up, the faster your thigh muscles will strengthen. This is, however, quite a challenge. And the higher you can curl your pelvis, the more you will be strengthening your inner thighs.

Do not strain your calves. If you feel a strain or pull in your calves when you are returning to the starting position, bend your arms and torso forward. After doing this scoop regularly you will soon be able to relax your calves without thinking about it.

FOR MORE OF A CHALLENGE:
Push your knees together when you are returning to the starting position.

DON'TS

- ❑ **Do not tense your body.**
- ❑ **Do not strain your arms forward, and keep your arms and shoulders relaxed.**
- ❑ **Do not uncurl your pelvis when you are returning to your original kneeling position.**
- ❑ **Do not arch your back when aiming your buttocks towards your heels.**
- ❑ **Do not let your buttocks untighten when you are returning to the kneeling position.**
- ❑ **Do not keep on going relentlessly. If you find yourself needing a breather, take one. Relax your body and breathe naturally. Then resume the original position and continue.**

L E G S

The Front-Thigh Stretch

THIS EXERCISE:

• STRETCHES THE NECK, PECTORAL MUSCLES, SPINE AND THIGHS •

• STRENGTHENS THE BUTTOCKS, INNER THIGHS AND STOMACH •

Technique

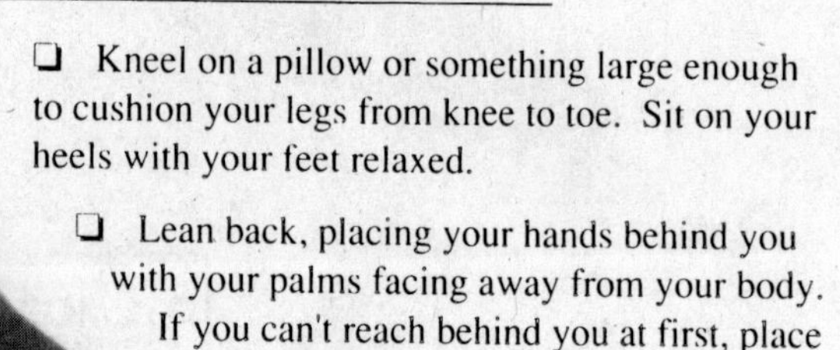

❑ Kneel on a pillow or something large enough to cushion your legs from knee to toe. Sit on your heels with your feet relaxed.

❑ Lean back, placing your hands behind you with your palms facing away from your body. If you can't reach behind you at first, place your hands by your sides. Rest your weight on your heels. Relax your neck.

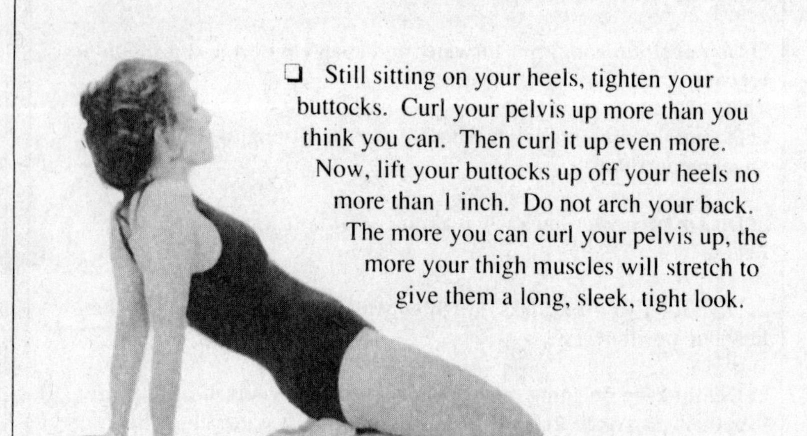

❑ Still sitting on your heels, tighten your buttocks. Curl your pelvis up more than you think you can. Then curl it up even more. Now, lift your buttocks up off your heels no more than 1 inch. Do not arch your back. The more you can curl your pelvis up, the more your thigh muscles will stretch to give them a long, sleek, tight look.

NOTE: The picture opposite, bottom is the starting position. Notice that there is less of a curve in the lower back and that the pubis bone can be seen in this picture. This shows how much the pelvis is curled up. Keep your knees together and your shoulders relaxed. Your pelvis should be curled up, even when sitting on your heels. It may be more comfortable for you in the beginning to separate your knees a wee bit.

Repetitions
WORK UP TO **10**

- ❑ Move you pelvis gently up and down no more than ¼ to ½ inch.

DON'TS
❑ **Do not arch your back. Keep your spine straight.**
❑ **Do not tense your neck.**
❑ **Do not move your head up or down.**
❑ **Do not forget to curl your pelvis up. The more you do this, the more your thighs will stretch.**
❑ **Do not put too much pressure on your hands and do not lock your elbows. Your arms should be straight but relaxed.**
❑ **Do not tense your body.**

The Inner-Thigh Squeeze

THIS EXERCISE:

• TIGHTENS THE INNER THIGHS •

• STRETCHES THE SPINE •

• STRENGTHENS THE STOMACH, BUTTOCKS, PSOAS, CALVES, AND FEET •

TECHNIQUE

Hold for a count of...
WORK UP TO **100**

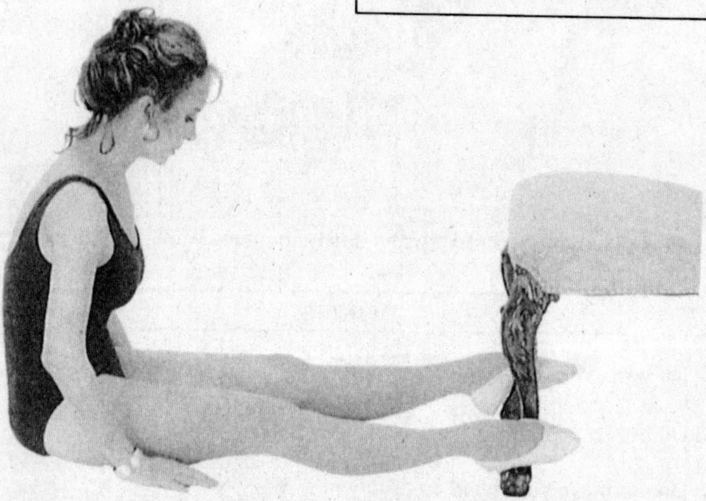

❑ Facing a sturdy chair or legs of a table, sit on the floor, your back straight. Your arms are at your sides, hands resting on the floor.

❑ Place the arch of each foot on the chair or table legs, which should be between 12 and 36 inches apart. Round and relax your upper torso so that you won't try to put pressure on your lower back.

❑ Keeping your toes pointed and relaxed, squeeze as if trying to bring the legs of your piece of furniture together. Your inner thighs are doing all the work. In the beginning, you will feel it in your calves and knees. Very soon, you will feel the power of your inner thighs working.

NOTE: If you find that your lower back is still assisting during the Inner-Thigh Squeeze, remember to keep your shoulders rounded. You can also take breather if you need to.
This is also a lovely opportunity to be able to stretch your neck. Let your head lower forward slightly, taking it down in a delicate, slow motion, until your chin is resting on your chest. Or, if you prefer, gently stretch your neck up towards the ceiling.

FOR MORE OF A CHALLENGE:

Place the arches of your feet as high as you can keep them without feeling a strain in your lower back.

FOR EVEN MORE OF A CHALLENGE:

With your legs resting on the floor, place the inside of your heels on the outside of the chair or table legs. Point your toes away from the chair or table legs, and squeeze with your heels.

DON'TS

- ❑ **Do not tense your shoulders, and keep your hands and arms relaxed and comfortable.**
- ❑ **Do not tense your legs.**
- ❑ **Do not lock your knees.**
- ❑ **Do not tense your lower back.**

BUILD YOUR STRENGTH

The following programme has been devised to help you slowly increase your strength if you find the Quick Callanetics programme too much for you at first.

The Waist-Away Stretch and the two Neck Relaxers act as a general warm up to loosen your body before moving on to the more specific exercises aimed at working your legs.

The Waist-Away Stretch

An alternative to wearing cinchers and corsets!

THIS EXERCISE:

• STRETCHES THE WAIST, SPINE, BACK OF THE SHOULDERS, AND UNDERARM AREA •

• REDUCES WAIST SIZE •

Technique

❑ Sit up straight in an armchair and allow your left arm to rest on the arm of the chair. (If you don't have an armchair, simply rest your left palm beside you on the seat of the chair.)

❑ Keeping the spine straight, slowly stretch your right arm up to the ceiling, palm facing inward. Try to keep your arm by your ear. You should feel the stretch from your waist right up to your underarm. Now, stretch up and try to reach even higher. Then start reaching over gently to the left side, trying to move your upper body and arm in the same direction, as if they were welded together.

❑ When you have reached over to the side as far as you can, move ¼ to ½ inch over and back. You should not be making any bouncing or jerking movements, and remember—move in triple slow motion.

❑ To reverse sides, or to come out of this exercise, slowly lower your arm and straighten your spine, until you have returned to the original position.

NOTE: If you feel any discomfort in your lower back, or if you have a swayback, you may want to try this exercise with your arms and torso bending slightly forward.

DON'TS

❑ **Do not bounce.**

❑ **Do not tense your shoulders or neck.**

❑ **Do not arch your lower back or stick out your stomach.**

Repetitions TO EACH SIDE			
Day1	Day2	Day3	Day4
25	30	40	50

The Neck Relaxer No. 1

A way to unlock tension.

THIS EXERCISE:

• LOOSENS THE NECK AND SHOULDERS •

• STRETCHES THE SPINE •

• INCREASES JOINT FLEXIBILITY •

• RELEASES TENSION IN THE NECK AND BETWEEN THE SHOULDER BLADES •

Technique

❑ Sit up straight in a chair or stand erect, feet a hip-width apart, knees bent, feet forward. Relax your shoulders—so much so that you feel they are sinking into the floor. Relax your entire body, being careful not to arch your back or stick out your buttocks.

❑ In triple slow motion, stretch your neck up. At the same time, lower your chin until it is resting on your chest. Relax your jaw. Relax your shoulders, and try to keep them even and back.

❑ Gently, leading with your chin, move your head towards your right shoulder until your nose is even with the middle of your shoulder. Now, look over your shoulder as far as possible, trying to stretch your neck even more. Hold for a slow count of 5.

DON'TS

❑ **Do not make any sharp or sudden movements; extreme moves can injure your neck.**

❑ **Do not hunch or tense your shoulders.**

❑ **Do not tense your jaw; it may help to keep your lips slightly apart.**

❑ **Do not lock your knees.**

❑ **Do not stick out your buttocks or stomach.**

❑ Neck still stretched, slowly bring your chin back down to your chest and move it towards your left shoulder in one continuous slow motion. Look over your left shoulder as far as possible, as on the right side, holding for a slow count of 5. Slowly, return your head to the centre. This sequence counts as one repetition.

Repetitions TO EACH SIDE			
Day1	Day2	Day3	Day4
2	3	4	5

The Neck Relaxer No. 2

Relaxation—plain and simple.

THIS EXERCISE:

• LOOSENS THE NECK AND SHOULDERS •

• STRETCHES THE SPINE •

• KEEPS THE NECK AREA FLEXIBLE •

Technique

❑ This exercise may be done sitting or standing.

❑ Sit up straight in a chair or stand erect, with your feet forward, a hip-width apart, knees bent. Relax your shoulders and arms.

❑ Stretch your neck up until you feel you can't stretch any higher. Look straight ahead and be conscious that you keep your jaw loose. Feel as if your shoulders were sinking right into the floor and as if a string were running from your head right to the ceiling, stretching your neck even more.

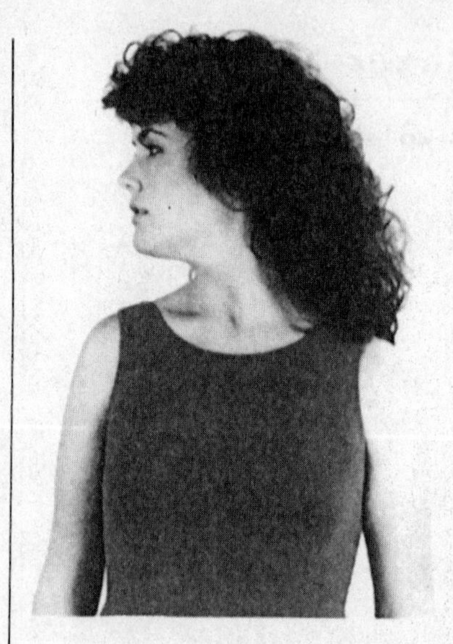

❑ Gently, in triple slow motion, turn your head as far as you can to the right until you feel a slight, comfortable stretch. Then, very slowly and in one continuous motion, move it to the left. Try to look over your shoulders, but be sure that you don't rotate them; they should remain facing front. A movement to both sides counts as one repetition.

DON'TS

❑ **Do not turn your body or rotate your shoulders.**

❑ **Do not lock your knees.**

❑ **Do not tense your neck or shoulders.**

❑ **Do not stick out your buttocks or your stomach.**

Repetitions TO EACH SIDE			
Day1	Day2	Day3	Day4
2	3	4	5

The Pelvic Wave

The way to leaner, longer-looking legs.

THIS EXERCISE:

• STRENGTHENS AND TIGHTENS THE LEGS, THE BUTTOCKS, AND THE ABDOMINAL MUSCLES •

• STRETCHES THE SPINE AND THE AREA BETWEEN THE SHOULDER BLADES •

• KEEPS THE PELVIS FLEXIBLE •

• WORKS THE FRONT AND INNER THIGHS, FEET, ANKLES, AND CALVES •

TECHNIQUE

❑ Face a barre. You may use the top of a table, counter, desk, back of a sofa, heavy chair, or anything that can support your weight. Whatever you use should not be lower than the middle of your thighs.

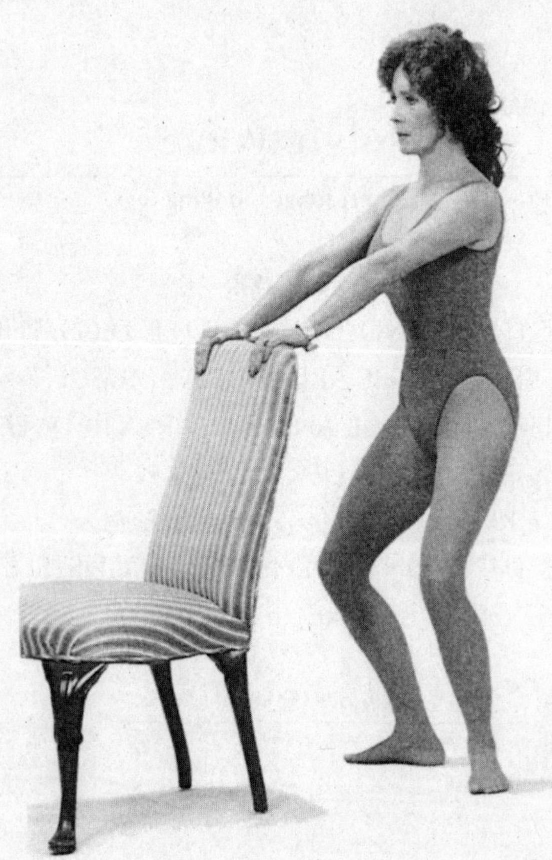

❑ Hold on to the barre with straight, yet relaxed arms. You should be about 12 to 18 inches away from your barre. Heels are a comfortable distance apart, knees bent, feet turned out. Relax your body totally.

DON'TS

❑ **Do not stick out your buttocks or stomach.**

❑ **Do not allow your buttocks to drop lower than your knees.**

❑ **Do not tense your shoulders.**

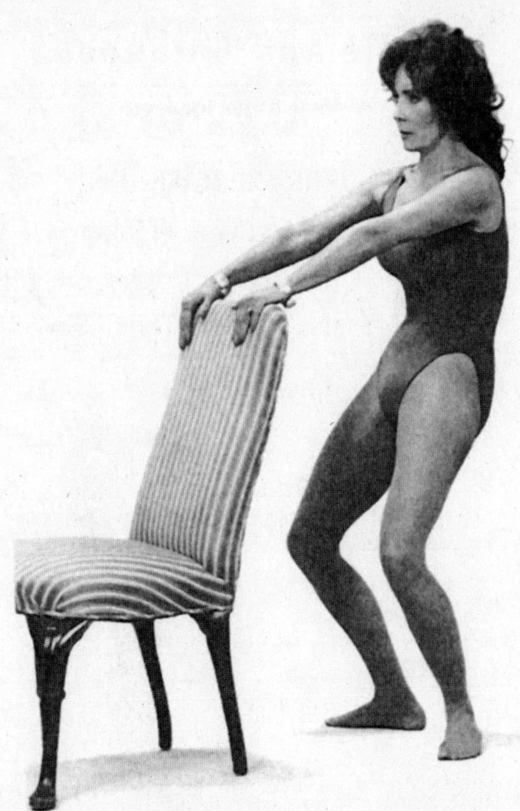

❑ Keeping your spine as straight as possible and shoulders back, bend your knees to lower your body 1 inch towards the floor. Then, in triple slow motion, tighten your buttocks and curl up your pelvis. With a little extra effort, you can curl up your pelvis even more than you think you can. Hold for a count 5, then slowly release your pelvis.

❑ Lower your body 1 inch more. Curl up your pelvis and hold for a count of 5, then slowly release it. Reverse the process: come back up 1 inch, curl your pelvis, and hold for another 5 counts, release, come up 1 inch more, curl your pelvis, hold for 5 and release. This entire sequence is one repetition.

Repetitions			
Day 1	Day 2	Day 3	Day 4
2	2	2	2

NOTE: At first you will not realize how much your pelvis can curl up with a beautiful, smooth flow. The more you relax your body, the easier this will be and the faster you will progress.

Plié and Balance

A great toner for legs.

THIS EXERCISE:

• STRENGTHENS AND TIGHTENS THE LEG MUSCLES, ESPECIALLY THOSE OF THE FRONT AND INNER THIGHS •

Technique

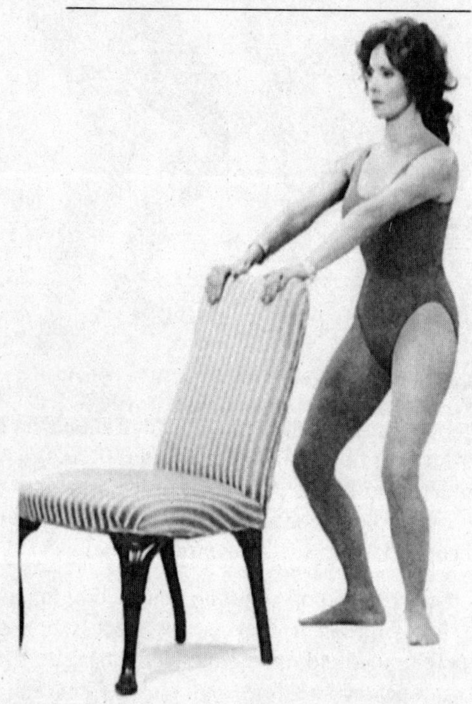

❑ Face the barre, standing about 12 to 18 inches away from it, and hold it with straight, yet relaxed arms. Your legs are relaxed, knees bent, feet flat on the floor, slightly turned out, a comfortable distance apart.

❑ In triple slow motion, gently bend your knees to lower your body as far as you can without having to lift your heels off the floor Trying to keep your body straight, your spine as erect as possible, return to the original position and repeat.

❑ Rather than holding the lowered position, try to make this one continuous up-and-down motion. But, remember—do it in triple slow motion.

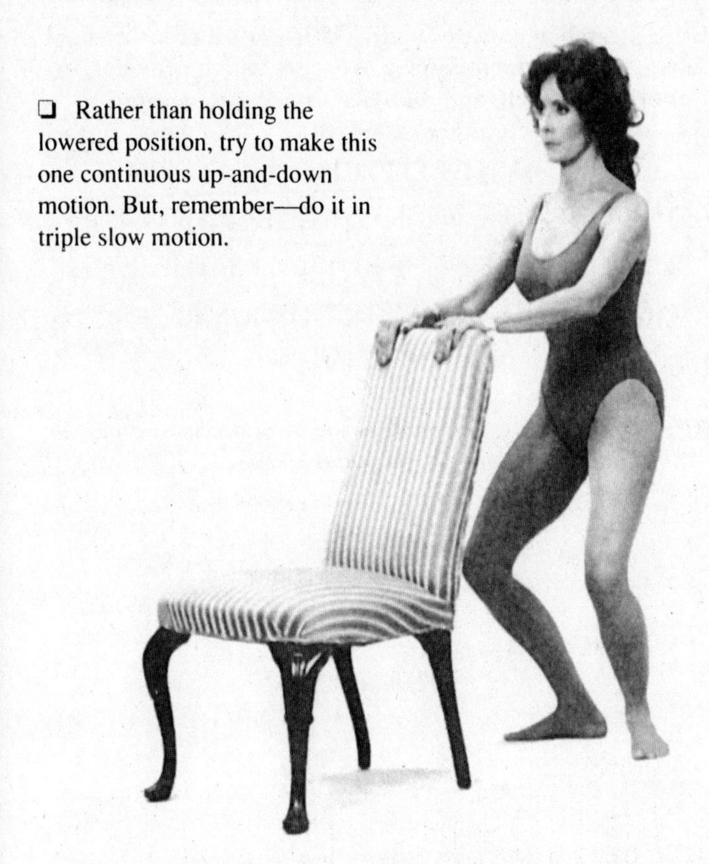

NOTE: If your leg muscles are weak, at first you may feel as if you are clinging to the barre with every muscle in your body. Even your teeth will feel as if they are trying to hold you up! As you gain strength in your legs, you will automatically be able to stand more erect and you will find yourself an arm's length away from the barre, with your hands only touching it lightly for balance.

Repetitions			
Day 1	Day 2	Day 3	Day 4
2	2	2	3

DON'TS

❑ **Do not stick out your buttocks or your stomach.**

❑ **Do not tense your shoulders.**

The Hamstring Stretch (Up and Over)

If this leg stretch aggravates your sciatica or other lower-back problems, skip to the following exercise, which provides an alternate stretch, and do twice as many repetitions as are called for.

THIS EXERCISE:

• STRETCHES THE NECK, SPINE, BETWEEN THE SHOULDER BLADES, THE BUTTOCKS, THE INNER THIGHS, THE HAMSTRING MUSCLES, AND THE CALVES •

NOTE: Find out what your limitations are by gently trying different positions and heights before you begin.

Technique

❑ For this exercise, whatever you are using as a barre should be even with or lower than your knee, such as a low chair or sofa.

❑ Face the barre and gently place your right heel on it, keeping the standing foot facing forward with the knee bent as much as possible. (You may have to turn the foot out slightly for balance.) Keep the raised right leg bent, and relax the standing leg as well.

❑ Place your hands, one in front of the other, on your right thigh. Hold your elbows out to the sides to stretch between your shoulder blades.

❑ In triple slow motion, your hands still resting on your thighs, move your torso towards your knee until you feel a stretch, then hold until you feel the muscles relax and you can stretch a little further.

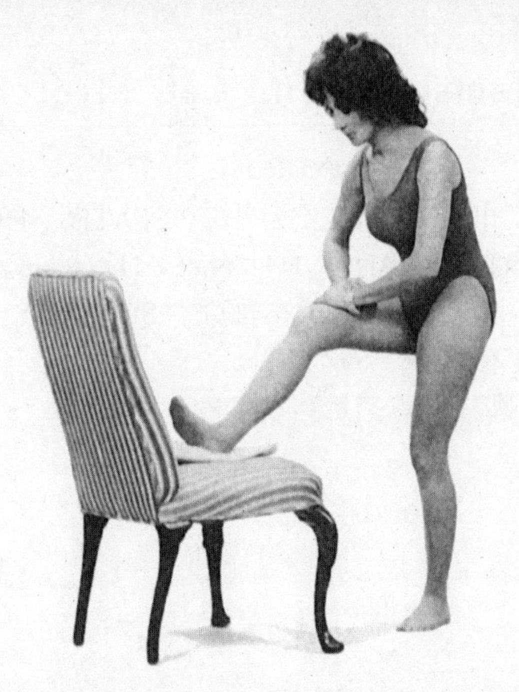

❑ Hold, then gently move the torso ¼ to ½ inch towards the knee and back. If you already feel a strong stretch, simply hold the position for the count. Keep your entire body relaxed, especially your neck and knees.

❑ To come out of this stretch, raise your torso, and gently, in triple slow motion, lift the leg off the barre and return it to the floor.

❑ Repeat with your left leg.

NOTE: If you want more of a stretch than you are able to get in this position, gently scoot the standing leg further back from the barre and try to straighten the raised leg as much as possible. If you find that the barre cuts into your ankle uncomfortably, cushion it with a thick cloth or towel.

Repetitions to each side			
Day 1	Day 2	Day 3	Day 4
15	15	20	20

DON'TS

❑ Do not lock either of your knees.

❑ Do not rest your hands on your knees.

❑ Do not make jerking movements with your neck or torso.

❑ Do not tense your neck or shoulders.

The Hamstring and Calf Stretch

THIS EXERCISE:

• STRETCHES THE NECK, SPINE, BETWEEN THE SHOULDER BLADES, THE INNER THIGHS, AND THE BACKS OF THE LEGS, ESPECIALLY THE HAMSTRINGS •

• STRENGTHENS THE PECTORAL MUSCLES •

TECHNIQUE

❑ Lie on your back, your entire body relaxed, knees bent, your feet flat on the floor a hip-width apart, a comfortable distance from your buttocks. Your arms are resting at your sides.

❑ Bend your right knee and, holding the back of your right thigh below the knee with both hands, elbows out to the side, bring your leg as close as possible toward your chin.

❑ Keeping your head on the floor, slowly straighten your leg as much as you can, aiming it upward without forcing it. Straighten it only as much as is comfortable.

❑ Hold for a count of 10 and then gently move your right leg towards you and back ¼ to ½ inch. It is very important that these delicate movements do not even resemble a bounce. If you really feel the stretch in your leg, simply hold for the count.

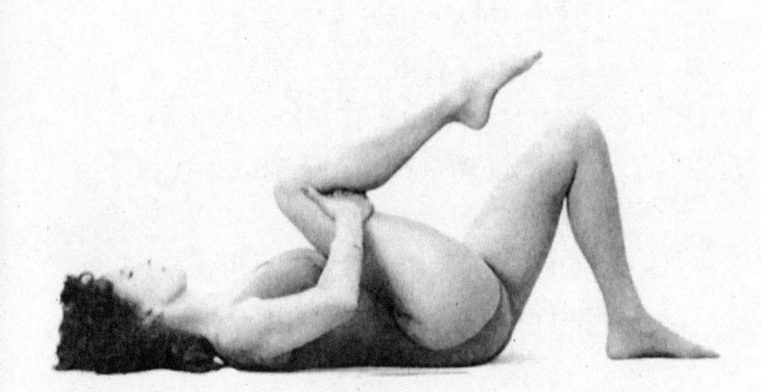

❑ To come out of this position, release your arms, and in triple slow motion return the raised leg to the starting position.

❑ Repeat to the left side.

NOTE: The hamstring muscle is usually the tightest muscle in the body. In fact, a large percentage of the population have extremely tight hamstrings. So be patient. It may take longer than thirty days to stretch this muscle completely. Just be aware that your muscles are stretching every time you do this exercise. And every little bit counts! As you become more flexible day by day, try to gradually increase the length of the count you hold the stretch from 10 to 30 seconds, before you begin the repetitions.

Repetitions TO EACH SIDE			
Day1	Day2	Day3	Day4
15	15	15	20

DON'TS

❑ **Do not bounce.**

❑ **Do not force the raised leg forward by pulling it.**

❑ **Do not force the raised leg to straighten.**

❑ **Do not tense your neck.**

The Pelvic Rotatio

This exercise and the next are based on a series I learned when studying belly dancing. Everyone loves to show off the flexibility they get from this one in particular. Try it, and you'll see that Elvis had the right idea.

THIS EXERCISE:

• STRENGTHENS THE BUTTOCKS, THIGHS, INNER THIGHS, LOWER BACK, STOMACH, AND PELVIC MUSCLES •

• STRETCHES THE ARMS AND SPINE •

• LOOSENS THE PELVIC AREA •

NOTE: Almost everyone finds this exercise difficult to do at first. This is because pelvic circles involve most of the muscle groups in your body. You've probably never even used some of them separately, never mind asking them to join together to do something they've never done before! So don't judge yourself; just do the best you can. Every time you do this exercise, you will be building strength in all these different muscles, and you will start to appreciate the benefits of this beautiful, flowing, seductive movement. Loosening the pelvic area is important. The legs and torso are influenced by it tremendously, and if this area is tight, you won't have the flexibility that everyone is entitled to. This exercise can help you regain the wonderful youthful suppleness and sense of freedom you had as a child.

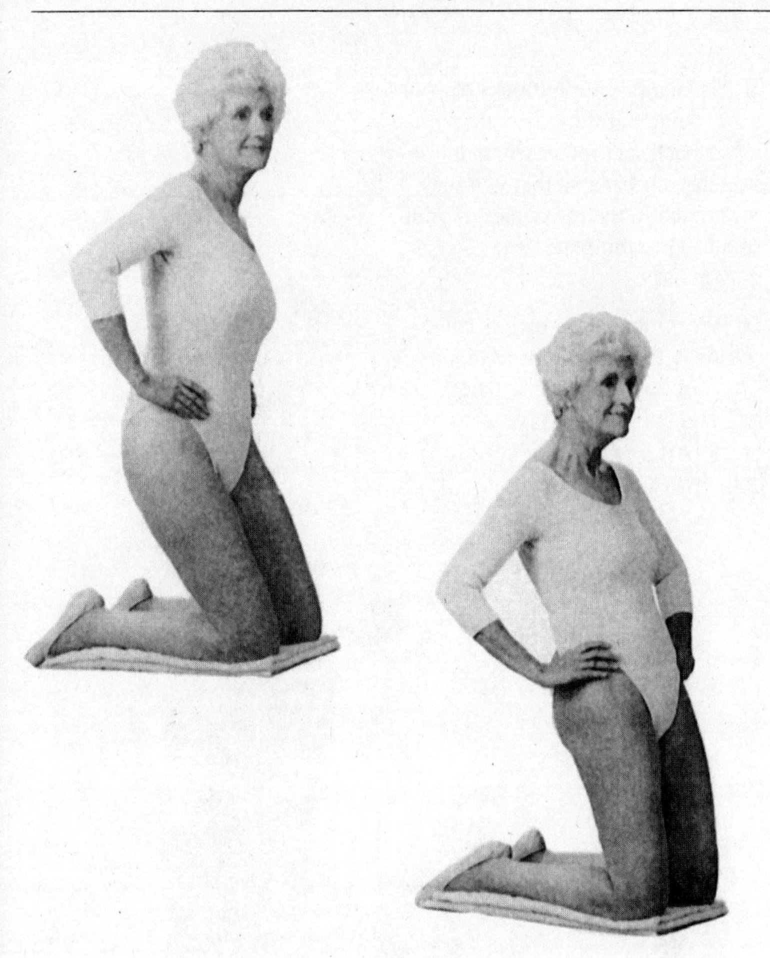

❑ Knees a hip-width apart, kneel on a pillow or something large enough to cushion your legs from knee to foot. Place your hands on your hips and lower your torso 3 inches.

❑ In triple slow motion, gently begin to move your hips (not your torso) as far as you can to the right. Then, slowly, rotate your pelvis to the front. Try to aim your pelvis up toward your navel, then slowly begin to rotate your hips as far as you can to the left side.

❑ Then aim your buttocks to your back, being careful not to arch your lower back, but rather trying to stretch your back so that you feel the stretch in the lower part of your spine. This completes one movement.

❑ Working at your own pace, complete the repetitions to this side, circling to the right, front, left, and back. Then take a breather if you feel you need it before reversing direction.

DONT'S

❑ **Do not arch your back.**

❑ **Do not stick out your stomach.**

❑ **Do not try to do too much too fast.**

Repetitions IN EACH DIRECTION			
Day1	Day2	Day3	Day4
2	2	2	2

The Pelvic Scoop

Graceful, flowing...beautifying.

THIS EXERCISE:

• STRENGTHENS THE LEG MUSCLES, ESPECIALLY THE FRONT AND INNER-THIGH MUSCLES, THE STOMACH, BUTTOCKS, AND CALVES •

• STRETCHES THE SPINE •

TECHNIQUE

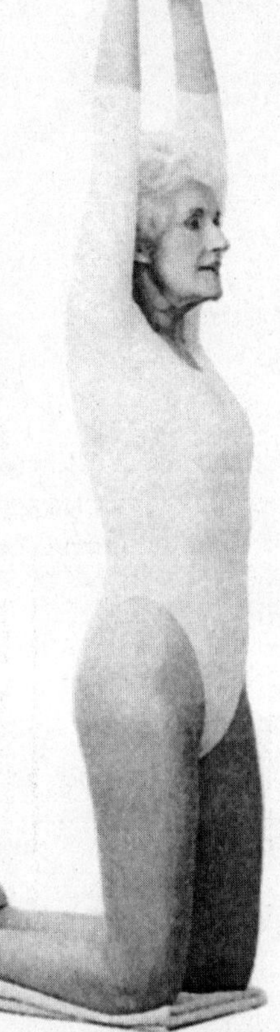

❑ Knees a hip-width apart, kneel on a pillow or something large enough to cushion your legs from knee to foot. Try to bring your arms straight up over your head, clasp your hands, and try to stretch your upper body, including your neck, as if you were trying to make your torso longer. Do this to the point where you can feel your lower back stretching.

❑ Continue to stretch as you slowly lower your buttocks about 4 inches, then tighten your buttock muscles and slowly curl up your pelvis. Hold this position for a count of three. Your arms will move forward when you tip the pelvis.

❑ In triple slow motion, still curling up your pelvis, use the strength of your thighs to lift your body back to the starting position. Try to keep stretching your spine as you do these slow, sinuous, powerful movements.

DON'TS

❑ **Do not arch your back.**

❑ **Do not jerk up your pelvis.**

Repetitions			
Day 1	Day 2	Day 3	Day 4
2	2	2	2

The Front-Thigh Stretch

For tight, slim, beautiful thighs.

THIS EXERCISE:

• STRETCHES THE NECK, PECTORAL MUSCLES, SPINE, AND THIGHS •

• STRENGTHENS THE BUTTOCKS, INNER THIGHS, AND STOMACH •

TECHNIQUE

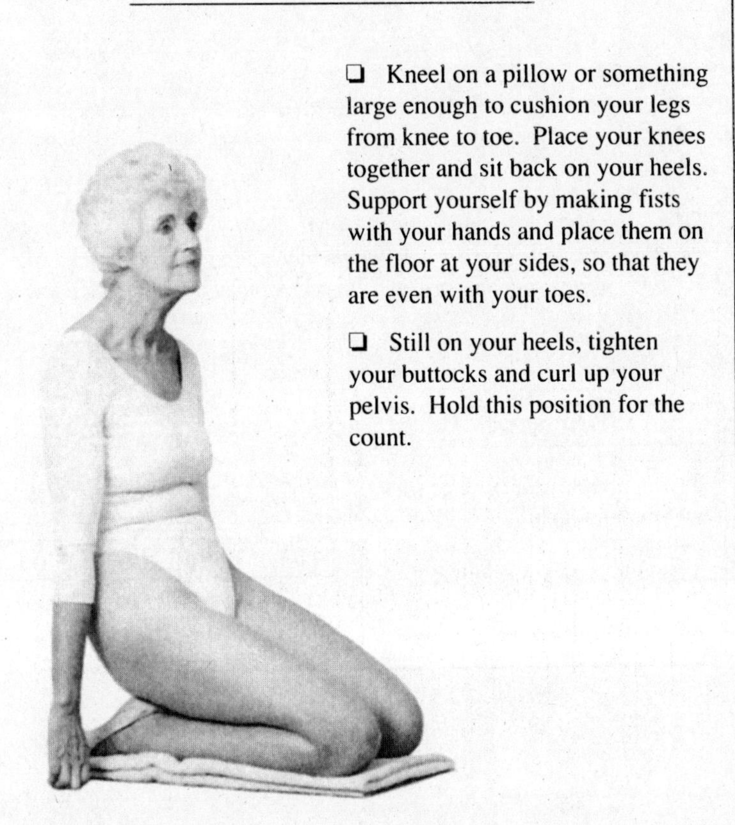

❑ Kneel on a pillow or something large enough to cushion your legs from knee to toe. Place your knees together and sit back on your heels. Support yourself by making fists with your hands and place them on the floor at your sides, so that they are even with your toes.

❑ Still on your heels, tighten your buttocks and curl up your pelvis. Hold this position for the count.

❑ Return to the original position by releasing your buttocks and, still sitting on your heels, using your fists to 'walk' yourself to an upright position. Relax.

NOTE: The more you can curl up your pelvis, the more you will stretch your thigh muscles. This stretch complements the pelvic exercises you have been doing, and will prevent the development of bulky muscles.

DON'TS

- ❑ **Do not arch your back or stick out your stomach.**
- ❑ **Do not tense your body.**
- ❑ **Do not hunch your shoulders.**

Hold for a count of...			
Day 1	Day 2	Day 3	Day 4
10	10	15	15

The Inner-Thigh Squeeze

As we get older, our inner thighs start to look like plastic bags filled with Jell-O. This exercise will give you lethal inner thighs.

THIS EXERCISE:

• TIGHTENS THE INNER THIGHS •

• STRETCHES THE SPINE •

• STRENGTHENS THE STOMACH, BUTTOCKS, PSOAS, CALVES, AND FEET •

NOTE: For this exercise, you will need something sturdy that you can squeeze with your legs. You can use a desk, a coffee or tea table, a chair—or even something like a filing cabinet. Its width is not critical, as long as you are comfortable. Just make sure that it's not fragile. You may be surprised at how strong your inner thighs will become as you do this powerful contraction.

TECHNIQUE

❑ Sit on the floor, in front of whatever you will be squeezing, your legs straight on the floor. Bend your knees and wrap the arches of your feet around the sides of the object.

❑ Next, round your upper back, allowing your shoulders to collapse and slouch slightly. Keep your arms relaxed, and rest your palms on the floor at your sides. If you try to sit up too fast too soon, you will be forcing your lower back to do much of the work.

❑ Keeping your knees bent, apply pressure with your feet and try to squeeze them together as hard as you can. Squeeze for the count, if you can, then release. You will see much better results if you squeeze continuously, instead of holding and relaxing.

NOTE: At first you may feel this exercise mostly in the calves and inside of the knees. As you progress, you'll feel it working the inner thighs.

DON'TS

❑ **Do not squeeze and release; hold steadily for the count.**

❑ **Do not tense your shoulders.**

Hold for a count of...			
Day 1	Day 2	Day 3	Day 4
25	25	25	25

Days 5-9

The Waist-Away Stretch

Technique

❑ Stand next to a barre (chair back, table, or dresser, for example) with feet a hip-width apart, facing forward, knees bent and relaxed. Rest your left hand or arm on the barre. Keeping your spine erect, slowly stretch your right arm upward, palm facing inward. Try to keep your arm by your ear.

❑ Still stretching upward, tighten your buttocks and curl up your pelvis. Then start reaching over to the left side. Complete the exercise as for Days 1-4, bending both knees deeply as you come out of the position. Work both sides.

NOTE: At first you may have to do this exercise bent slightly forward, and you may not be able to keep the raised arm straight or by your ear. As you get stronger, your torso will be able to stretch over to the side more, and instead of just feeling the stretch in your waist, you will feel it from your hip to your hand!

DON'TS

- ❑ **Do not bounce.**
- ❑ **Do not tense your shoulders or neck.**
- ❑ **Do not arch your lower back or stick out your stomach.**
- ❑ **Do not lock your knees.**

Repetitions
TO EACH SIDE

Day 5	Day 6	Day 7	Day 8	Day 9
30	40	50	60	75

The Neck Relaxer No. 1

TECHNIQUE

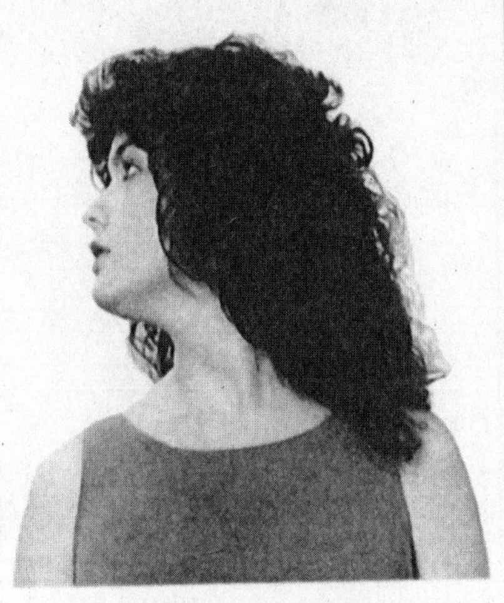

DON'TS

- ❑ **Do not make any sharp or sudden movements.**
- ❑ **Do not hunch or tense your shoulders.**
- ❑ **Do not tense your jaw.**
- ❑ **Do not lock your knees.**
- ❑ **Do not stick out your stomach or arch your back.**

❑ Repeat as for Days 1-4. If you have been doing this exercise sitting down, now do it standing, with knees bent. As your muscles relax and become stretched you will find that you can stretch further without tensing your shoulders.

Repetitions TO EACH SIDE				
Day 5	Day 6	Day 7	Day 8	Day 9
5	5	5	5	5

The Neck Relaxer No. 2

TECHNIQUE

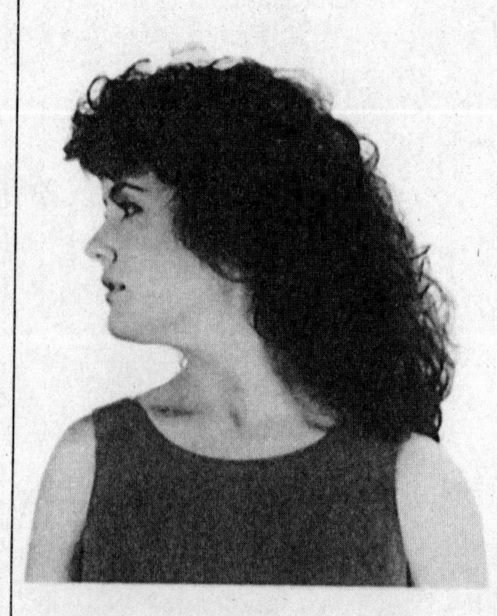

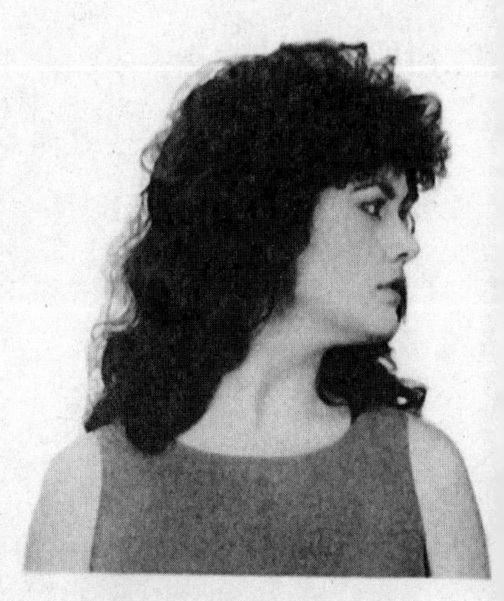

❑ Repeat as for Days 1-4. If you have been doing this exercise sitting down, now do it standing, with knees bent.

NOTE: As your body learns to relax, you will be able to perform these movements more smoothly.

DON'TS

❑ **Do not turn your body or rotate your shoulders.**

❑ **Do not lock your knees.**

❑ **Do not tense your neck or shoulders.**

❑ **Do not stick out your buttocks or stomach.**

Repetitions TO EACH SIDE				
Day 5	Day 6	Day 7	Day 8	Day 9
5	5	5	5	5

The Pelvic Wave

TECHNIQUE

❑ Repeat as for Days 1-4, but this time raise your heels off the floor about 1 to 2 inches, keeping your legs apart, feet turned out slightly for balance. In addition, instead of lowering your body and curling up your pelvis just 2 times, now go down 3 times and back up 3 times. This again is one repetition.

NOTE: By now, you should be able to curl up your pelvis further. With even ¼ of an inch more, you'll feel an incredible difference. When lowering your body, you should try to keep your torso erect. However, when you start to curl up your pelvis, aiming your pubic bone more into the navel, your upper back will automatically start to round. Allow this to happen—it's a thrilling development—for now you are not only tightening your legs and inner thighs, but you're also getting a wonderful, tension-releasing stretch in your spine.

DON'TS

❑ **Do not stick out your buttocks or stomach.**

❑ **Do not allow your buttocks to drop lower than your knees.**

❑ **Do not let your heels drop to the floor.**

❑ **Do not tense your shoulders.**

Repetitions				
Day5	Day6	Day7	Day8	Day9
3	3	3	3	3

Plié and Balance

Technique

❑ Repeat as for Days 1-4, but this time raise your heels 2 inches off the floor, keeping your legs apart, feet turned out slightly for balance. In triple slow motion, lower your body 2 inches and return to the starting position, with your knees bent, your heels off the floor.

NOTE: Those of you with ballet training may recognize this movement. It is, indeed, a standard ballet plié that I have modified slightly. However, even if you have had ballet lessons, you may find it difficult to do at first.

DON'TS

❑ Do not stick out your buttocks or your stomach.

❑ Do not drop your heels, going down or coming back up.

❑ Do not tense your shoulders.

Repetitions				
Day5	Day6	Day7	Day8	Day9
3	3	4	4	5

The Hamstring Stretch (Up and Over)

Technique

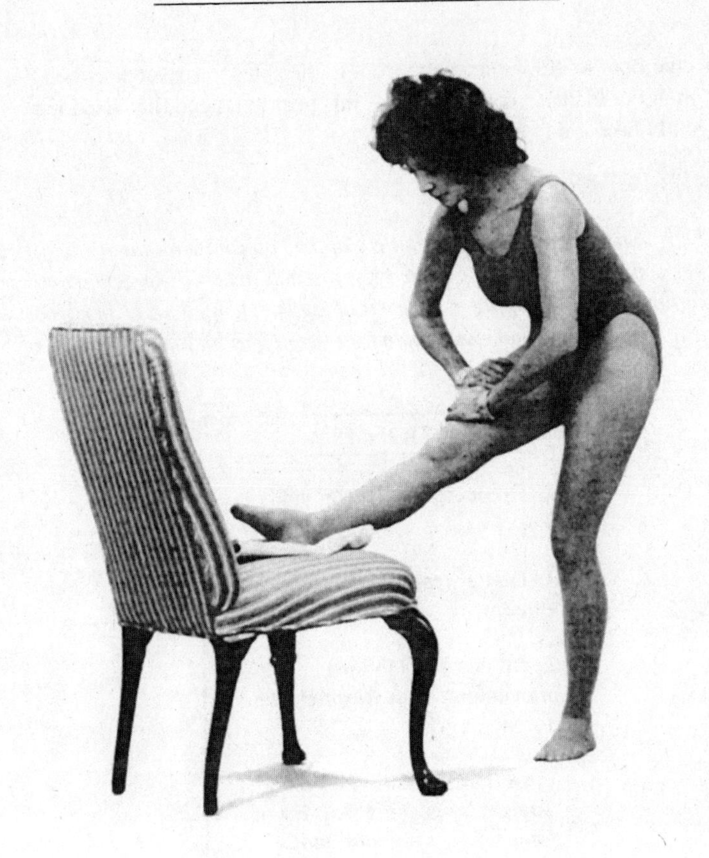

❑ Repeat as for Days 1-4, but this time try to straighten the knee of the raised leg. If you are able, try lifting your leg onto a higher barre. (If you can't find a suitable higher surface, simply scoot the standing leg back further.)

❑ Remember to hold your elbows out to the sides to stretch between your shoulder blades. To come out of this position, bend the raised leg and gently take it down.

❑ Work both sides.

NOTE: If you are one of those people who has puffiness on the inside of the knees, simply rotating the raised leg when doing this exercise can help tighten it. For example, if your right leg is extended on your barre, turn it to the right and this will extend the stretch to include the inside of the knee.

DON'TS

❑ Do not lock either of your knees.

❑ Do not rest your hands on your knee.

❑ Do not make jerking movements with your neck or torso.

❑ Do not force the raised leg straight by pushing your leg or knee down with your hands.

❑ Do not tense your neck or shoulders.

Repetitions
TO EACH SIDE

Day 5	Day 6	Day 7	Day 8	Day 9
25	25	30	30	30

The Hamstring and Calf Stretch

TECHNIQUE

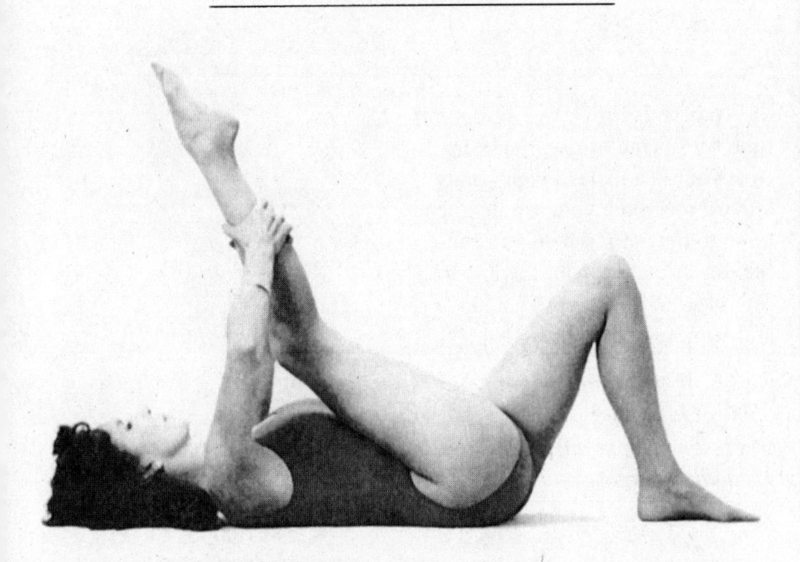

❑ Repeat as for Days 1-4, but this time hold on to your calf instead of your thigh, and extend your elbows even further out to the side to stretch between your shoulder blades. Try to straighten your leg if you can. Hold for a count of 30 before you begin your repetitions.

❑ Work both sides.

NOTE: As you become more proficient, you will be able to extend your elbows further and further out to the side. You will also be able to bring your legs closer and closer to your chin, but be patient—don't force it.

DON'TS

❑ **Do not bounce.**

❑ **Do not force the raised leg forward by pulling it.**

❑ **Do not force the raised leg to straighten.**

❑ **Do not tense your neck.**

Repetitions
TO EACH SIDE

Day 5	Day 6	Day 7	Day 8	Day 9
20	20	20	25	25

The Pelvic Rotation

TECHNIQUE

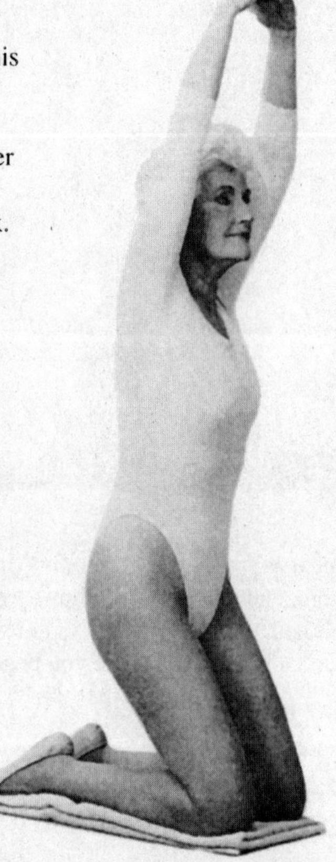

❑ Repeat as for Days 1-4, but this time bring your arms straight up over your head, clasp your hands and try to stretch your whole upper torso to the point where you can feel the stretch in your lower back. Then lower your body 6 inches, and continue as for Days 1-4.

NOTE: When you begin, do these motions in triple slow motion. As you become more adept, you can gradually increase your pace.

DONT'S

❑ **Do not arch your back.**

❑ **Do not stick out your stomach.**

❑ **Do not try to do too much too fast.**

Repetitions
IN EACH DIRECTION

Day 5	Day 6	Day 7	Day 8	Day 9
3	3	3	3	3

The Pelvic Scoop

TECHNIQUE

- ❑ From the starting position, stretch your arms and torso as for Days 1-4. Continue to stretch as you aim your buttocks toward your heels. Round and lean your torso forward while slowly lowering your buttocks as if you were going to sit down. Aim toward your heels and make sure you do not arch your back.

- ❑ Lower yourself about 6 to 8 inches, then tighten your buttock muscles and slowly curl up your pelvis. Return to the starting position using the strength of your thighs as for Days 1-4.

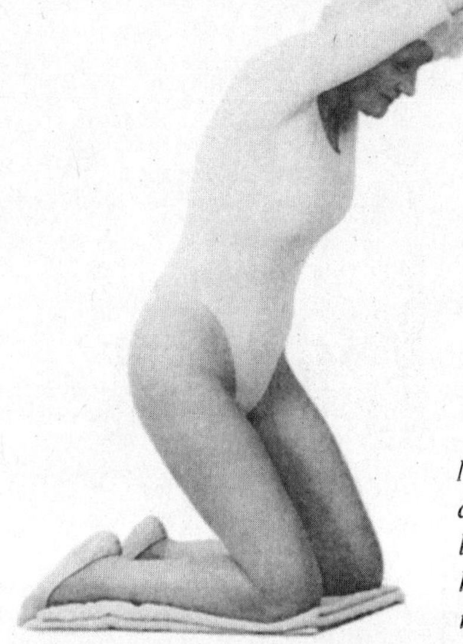

NOTE: As you become more adept at this exercise, you won't have to lean forward and will be able to keep your shoulders back even more as you come up.

Repetitions				
Day5	Day6	Day7	Day8	Day9
3	3	3	3	3

DON'TS

- ❑ **Do not arch your back.**
- ❑ **Do not jerk up your pelvis.**

L
E
G
S

The Front-Thigh Stretch

Technique

- ❑ Repeat as for Days 1-4, but this time, instead of making fists with your hands, try to place your palms on the floor behind you.

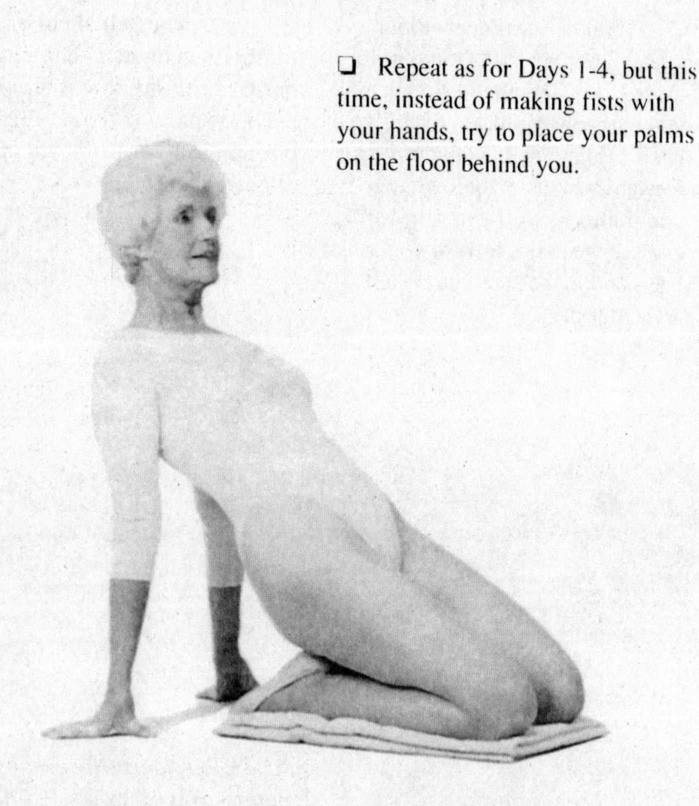

DON'TS

- ❑ Do not arch your back or stick out your stomach.
- ❑ Do not tense your body.
- ❑ Do not hunch your shoulders.

NOTE: This movement will seem easier if you try to stay conscious of relaxing your entire body as you do it.

Hold for a count of...				
Day5	Day6	Day7	Day8	Day9
20	20	20	20	20

The Inner-Thigh Squeeze

TECHNIQUE

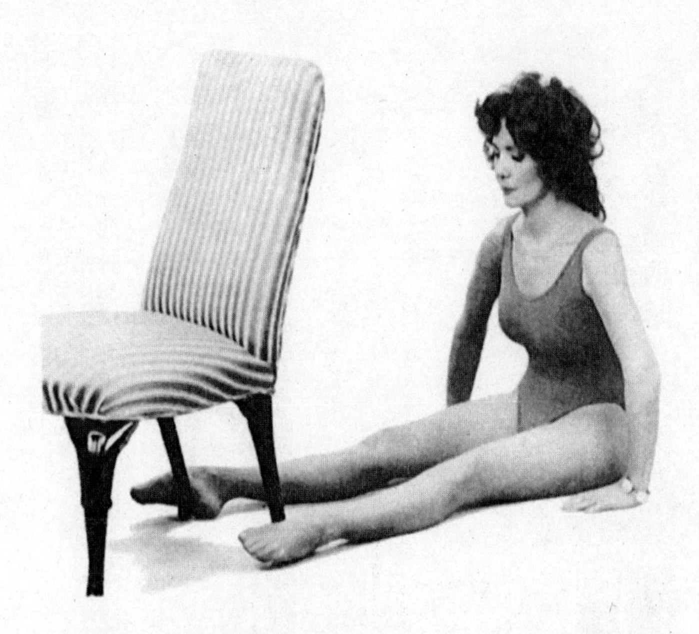

- ❑ Repeat as for Days 1-4, but this time try to straighten your legs.

NOTE: As your muscles gain strength, you will find that you can do this exercise sitting more erect, but it's very important to stay relaxed.

Hold for a count of...				
Day5	Day6	Day7	Day8	Day9
50	50	50	50	50

DON'TS

- ❑ **Do not squeeze and release; hold steadily for the count.**
- ❑ **Do not tense your shoulders.**
- ❑ **Do not lock your knees.**

Days 10-16

The Waist-Away Stretch

Technique

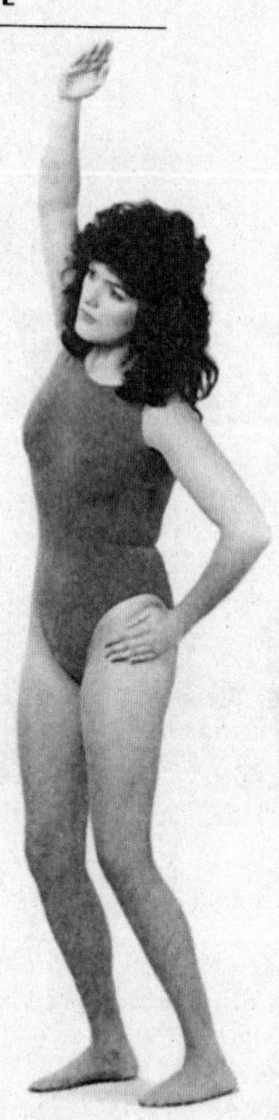

❑ Repeat as for Days 5-9, but this time, instead of resting your arm on a barre, support yourself by placing your hand just below your hip, your elbow pointing straight out to the side, if possible, and straighten your knees a bit.

❑ Slowly stretch your other arm upward, palm facing inward. Stretch up and over to the side, trying to move your upper body and arm together. You may bend slightly forward if necessary. Continue as for Days 5-9.

❑ To reverse sides, keep your hand on your hip and bend your knees even more. Continue to stretch the right arm over, and continue around to the front, slowly extending your arm down and then over to the right side in a slow sweeping movement. Coming out of the stretch in this way prevents putting pressure on the lower back.

❑ Tighten your buttocks, curl up your pelvis, and slowly straighten your spine, vertebra by vertebra, as you lower the arm. Repeat the exercise on the left side. When you have completed the left side, come out of the exercise as above.

NOTE: At first you may have trouble keeping your arm fully extended and curling your pelvis up.

DON'TS

- ❑ **Do not bounce.**
- ❑ **Do not tense your shoulders or neck.**
- ❑ **Do not arch your lower back or stick out your stomach.**
- ❑ **Do not let your resting elbow point forward or backward.**
- ❑ **Do not lock your knees.**

Repetitions
TO EACH SIDE

Day 10	Day 11	Day 12	Day 13	Day 14	Day 15	Day 16
50	50	55	60	65	70	75

The Neck Relaxer No. 1

TECHNIQUE

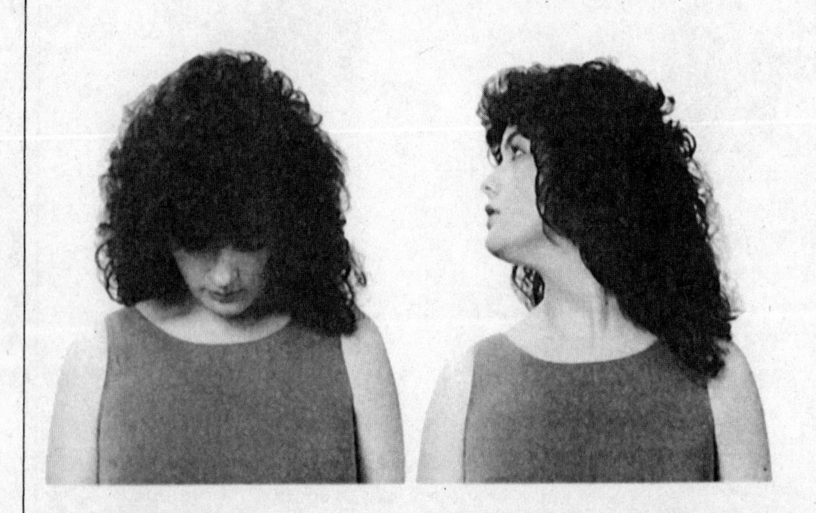

DON'TS

❑ Do not make any sharp or sudden movements.

❑ Do not hunch or tense your shoulders.

❑ Do not tense your jaw.

❑ Do not lock your knees.

❑ Do not stick out your buttocks or stomach.

❑ Repeat as for Days 5-9, but this time, at the same time, curl up your pelvis as far as you can, to stretch your spine.

Repetitions TO EACH SIDE						
Day 10	Day 11	Day 12	Day 13	Day 14	Day 15	Day 16
3	3	3	3	3	3	3

The Neck Relaxer No. 2

TECHNIQUE

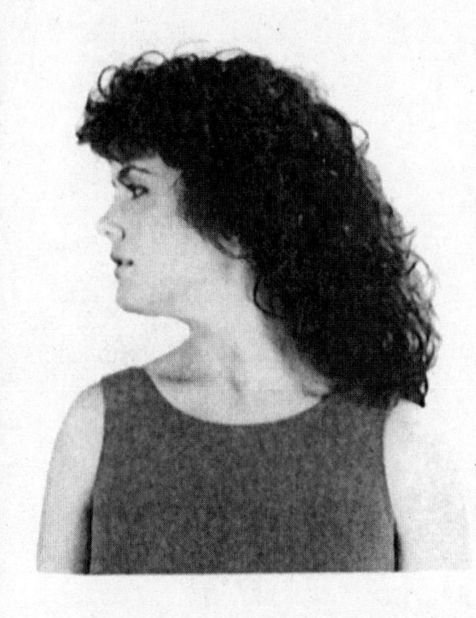

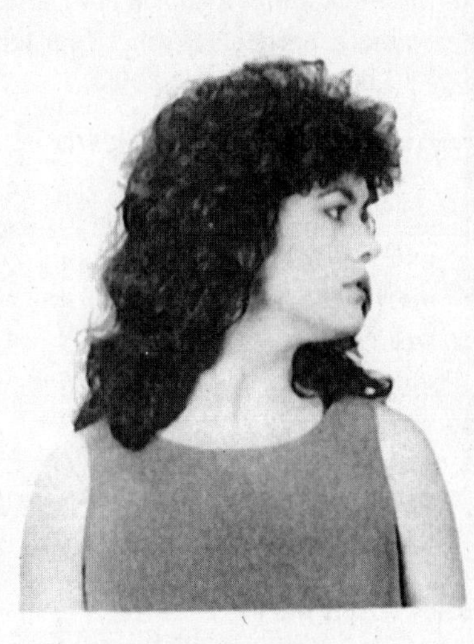

❑ Repeat as for Days 5-9, but this time, at the same time, curl up your pelvis as far as you can, to stretch your spine.

Repetitions TO EACH SIDE						
Day 10	Day 11	Day 12	Day 13	Day 14	Day 15	Day 16
5	5	5	5	5	5	5

DON'TS

❑ **Do not turn your body or rotate your shoulders.**

❑ **Do not lock your knees.**

❑ **Do not tense your shoulders.**

❑ **Do not stick out your buttocks or stomach.**

The Pelvic Wave

TECHNIQUE

❑ Repeat as for Days 5-9, but raise your heels off the floor 3 to 4 inches and move your feet together so that your heels touch. Your feet will be slightly turned out.

NOTE: With your heels off the floor, at first you may find it difficult to curl up your pelvis. You will gradually get better at this movement, and this will start to stretch your spine and work your inner thighs more. Your balance will also improve, and you won't feel that you need to clutch the barre using every muscle in your body.

DON'TS

- **❑ Do not stick out your buttocks or stomach.**
- **❑ Do not allow your buttocks to drop lower than your knees.**
- **❑ Do not let your heels drop to the floor.**
- **❑ Do not tense your shoulders.**

Repetitions

Day10	Day11	Day12	Day13	Day14	Day15	Day16
4	4	4	4	4	4	4

Plié and Balance

Technique

❑ Repeat as for Days 5-9, but this time raise your heels 2 to 3 inches off the floor and then move your feet together so that your heels touch. Turn out your feet so that your knees are over your toes. This time, in triple slow motion, lower your body 4 inches.

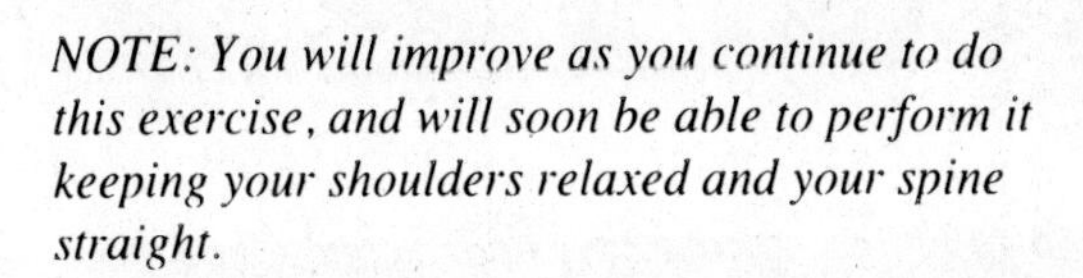

NOTE: You will improve as you continue to do this exercise, and will soon be able to perform it keeping your shoulders relaxed and your spine straight.

Repetitions						
Day10	Day11	Day12	Day13	Day14	Day15	Day16
5	5	6	6	6	7	7

DON'TS

❑ Do not stick out your buttocks or your stomach.

❑ Do not drop your heels, going down or coming up.

❑ Do not tense your shoulders.

The Hamstring Stretch (Up and Over)

Technique

- ❑ Repeat as for Days 5-9, using a higher barre (but only as high as is comfortable) and continuing to try to straighten your raised leg. Concentrate on letting your entire body melt.
- ❑ Work both sides.

NOTE: To make your barre higher, all you have to do is put a thick book (like a dictionary) or a firm throw pillow on top of what you were using. Just be sure it won't slip. You may also simply choose another piece of furniture to use.

At first it may be difficult to keep your standing foot facing to the front. In order to maintain your balance, you may have to turn the foot a little to the side. As you get better at this stretch, you will be able to keep it facing forward, rather than turned out.

DON'TS

- ❑ Do not lock either of your knees.
- ❑ Do not rest your hands on your knees.
- ❑ Do not make jerking movements with your neck or torso.
- ❑ Do not force the raised leg straight by pushing your leg or knee down with your hands.
- ❑ Do not tense your neck or shoulders.
- ❑ Do not attempt a greater height than is comfortable.

Repetitions
TO EACH SIDE

Day 10	Day 11	Day 12	Day 13	Day 14	Day 15	Day 16
30	35	35	35	35	40	40

The Hamstring and Calf Stretch

TECHNIQUE

❑ Repeat as for Days 5-9, but this time, if you can straighten your leg, hold on to your ankle for more of a stretch. If you are not stretched enough for this, continue to hold on to your calf. Try to straighten your raised leg even more toward your chest.

❑ Work both sides.

NOTE: If your muscles are stretched enough, you can try to flex the toes on your raised foot. This will stretch your calf muscle as well.

Repetitions TO EACH SIDE						
Day 10	Day 11	Day 12	Day 13	Day 14	Day 15	Day 16
25	30	30	30	35	35	35

DON'TS

❑ **Do not bounce.**

❑ **Do not force the raised leg forward by pulling it.**

❑ **Do not force the raised leg to straighten.**

❑ **Do not tense your neck.**

The Pelvic Rotation

Technique

❑ Knees together, sit back on your heels, keeping your spine straight. Bring your arms over your head as for Days 5-9. Now, lift your body straight up about 4 inches off your heels, or higher if you have to. Continue to rotate your pelvis as for Days 1-4. Repeat in the opposite direction.

NOTE: It is important to remember to work at your own pace, taking breathers whenever you need them.

Repetitions IN EACH DIRECTION						
Day 10	Day 11	Day 12	Day 13	Day 14	Day 15	Day 16
4	4	4	4	4	4	4

DON'TS

❑ Do not arch your back.

❑ Do not stick out your stomach.

❑ Do not try too much too fast.

The Pelvic Scoop

TECHNIQUE

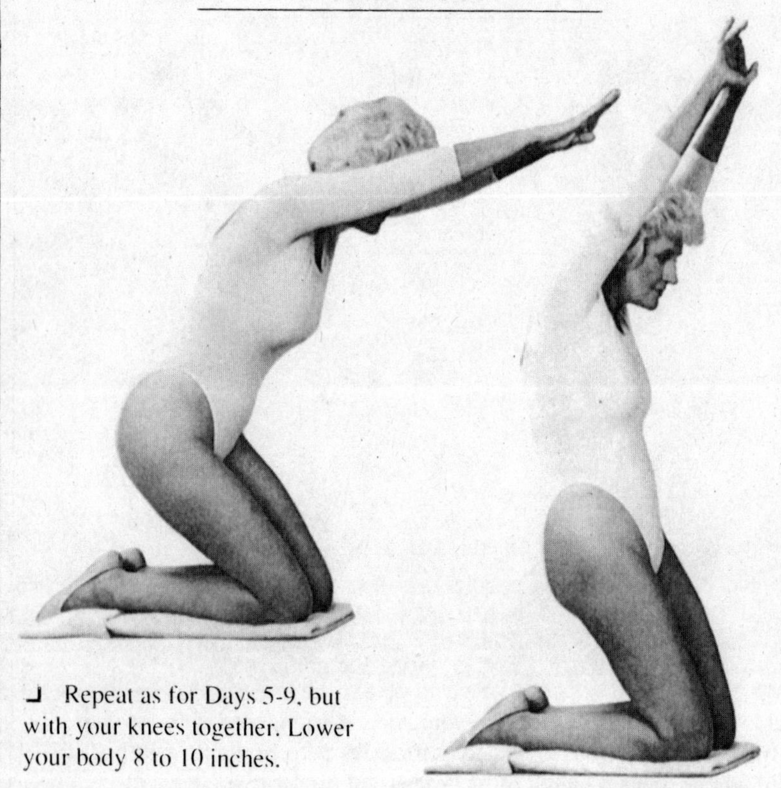

- Repeat as for Days 5-9, but with your knees together. Lower your body 8 to 10 inches.

NOTE: As you become more adept at this exercise, your movements will become more fluid. You will be able to keep your knees together easily and learn to relax your calf muscles.

DON'TS

- **Do not arch your back.**
- **Do not jerk up your pelvis.**

Repetitions						
Day 10	Day 11	Day 12	Day 13	Day 14	Day 15	Day 16
4	4	4	4	4	4	4

The Front-Thigh Stretch

TECHNIQUE

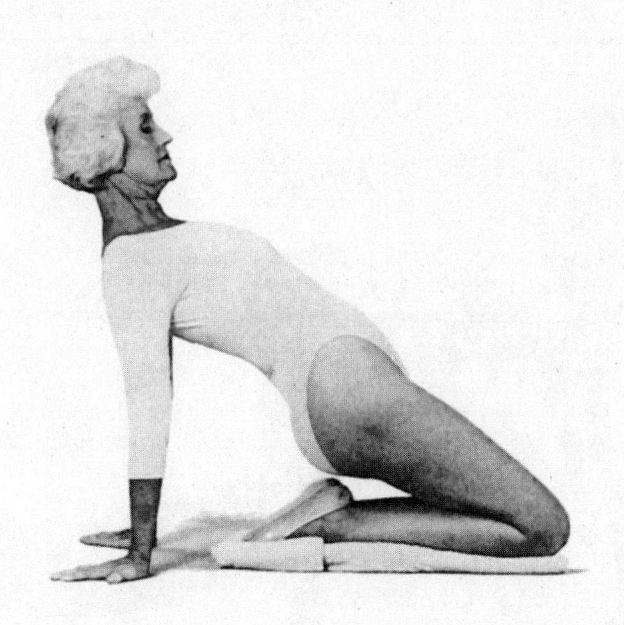

❑ Repeat as for Days 5-9. When you have stretched enough to feel a slight pull in the front of your thighs, curl up your pelvis even more and lift your buttocks off your heels, no more than 1 inch at first. Hold this position for the count.

❑ Relax your buttocks and gently return to the starting position, sitting on your heels. Relax your entire body.

Hold for a count of...						
Day 10	Day 11	Day 12	Day 13	Day 14	Day 15	Day 16
20	20	20	20	20	20	20

DON'TS

❑ **Do not arch your back or stick out your stomach.**

❑ **Do not allow your head to drop back.**

❑ **Do not tense your body.**

❑ **Do not hunch your shoulders or tense your neck.**

The Inner-Thigh Squeeze

Technique

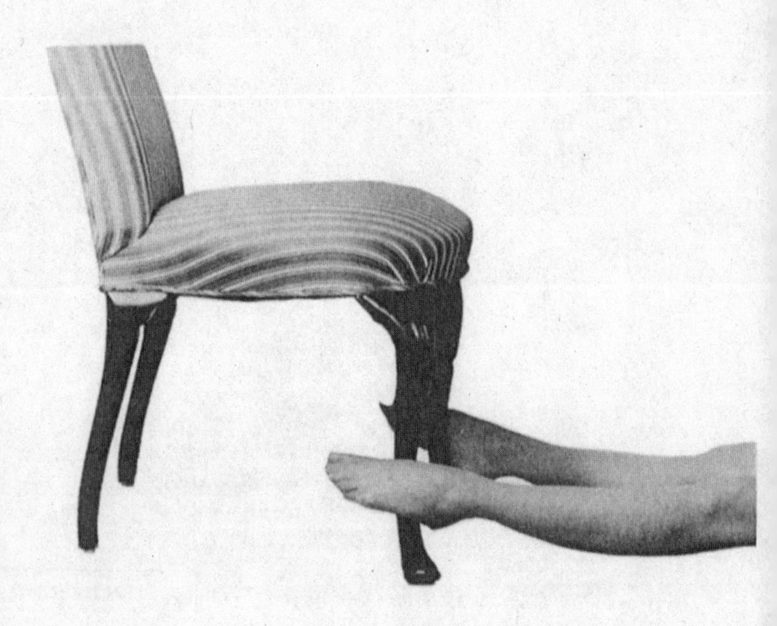

DON'TS

❑ **Do not squeeze and release; hold steadily for the count.**

❑ **Do not tense your shoulders.**

❑ **Do not lock your knees.**

❑ Repeat as for Days 5-9, lifting your feet 1 to 4 inches off the floor, as is comfortable, and continuing to try to keep your legs straight.

NOTE: When doing this exercise, if your feet keep slipping, try removing your socks. Bare feet won't slide as much.

Hold for a count of...						
Day 10	Day 11	Day 12	Day 13	Day 14	Day 15	Day 16
75	75	75	75	75	75	75

Days 17-30

The Waist-Away Stretch

Technique

- ❑ Repeat as for Days 10-16, standing straight and tightening your buttocks and curling up the pelvis even more before you start reaching over to the side. Try to hold your extended arm by your ear.
- ❑ Work both sides.

NOTE: As your muscles get stronger, you will find that you can curl up your pelvis and bend over to the side even more. You will gradually be able to straighten your legs, still keeping them relaxed, and you will be able to keep your arm straight and by your ear. You will also become even more conscious of the wonderful stretch in your spine.

Repetitions TO EACH SIDE

Day 17	Day 18	Day 19	Day 20	Day 21	Day 22	Days 23-30
60	70	75	75	75	75	75

DON'TS

- ❑ **Do not bounce.**
- ❑ **Do not tense your shoulders or neck.**
- ❑ **Do not arch your lower back or stick out your stomach.**
- ❑ **Do not let your resting elbow point forward or backward.**
- ❑ **Do not lock your knees.**

The Neck Relaxer No. 1

Technique

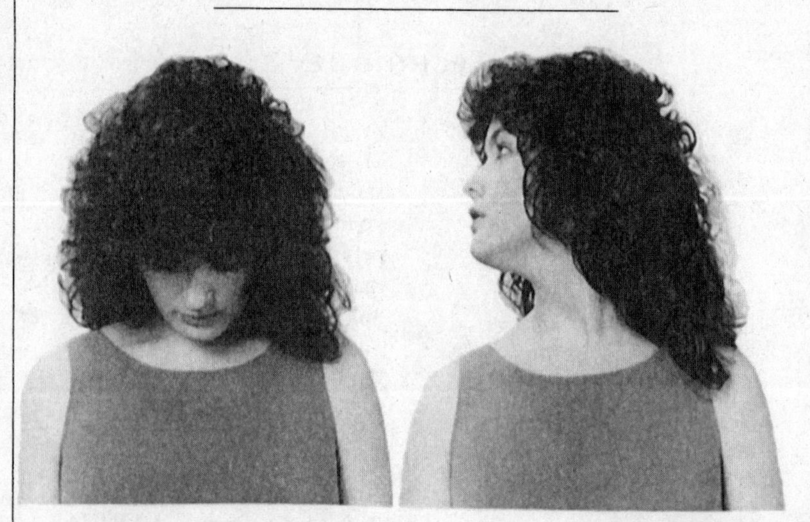

❑ Repeat as for Days 10-16, trying to curl up your pelvis even more, and without bending your knees as much.

Repetitions TO EACH SIDE						
Day 17	Day 18	Day 19	Day 20	Day 21	Day 22	Days 23-30
5	5	5	5	5	5	5

DON'TS

❑ Do not make any harsh or sudden movements.

❑ Do not hunch or tense your shoulders.

❑ Do not tense your jaw.

❑ Do not lock your knees.

❑ Do not stick out your stomach or arch your back.

The Neck Relaxer No. 2

TECHNIQUE

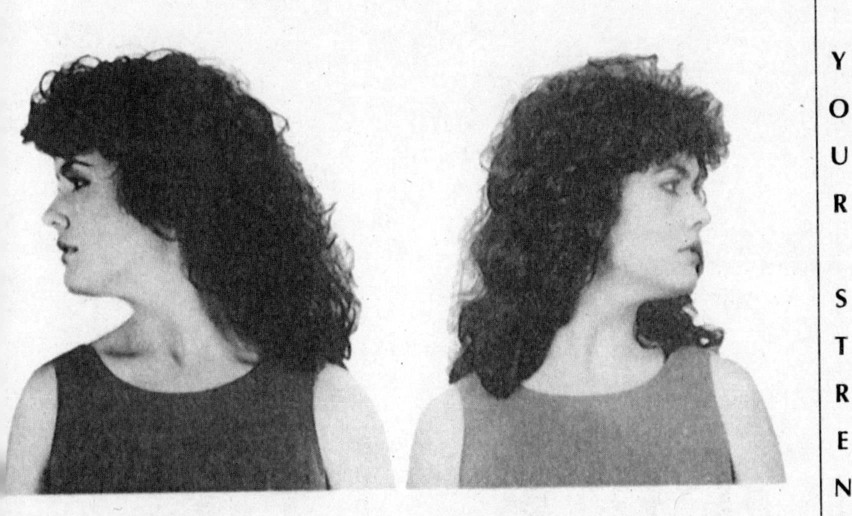

DON'TS

❑ **Do not turn your body or rotate your shoulders.**

❑ **Do not lock your knees.**

❑ **Do not tense your neck or shoulders.**

❑ **Do not stick out your buttocks or stomach.**

❑ Repeat as for Days 10-16.

NOTE: As your muscles relax even more, you will be able to curl up your pelvis more to stretch your spine and you won't have to bend your knees as much.

Repetitions TO EACH SIDE						
Day 17	Day 18	Day 19	Day 20	Day 21	Day 22	Days 23-30
5	5	5	5	5	5	5

The Pelvic Wave

Technique

❑ Repeat as for Days 10-16, lifting your heels as high as you can, so that you are balancing on the balls of your feet, heels together. Go smoothly from one position to the next without holding for the count, as you will be getting double the contraction in this position. If you are able, you may go 1 or 2 inches lower, but don't let your buttocks drop lower than your knees, or you will put a terrific strain on your knees.

NOTE: As you gain strength, the tension in your body will begin to disappear. You will also be astonished at how far you are able to curl up your pelvis. As the muscles in your legs, toes, feet, ankles and calves become stronger you will be able to go down even lower working the buttock and stomach muscles even more.

As this happens, this exercise will feel easier and easier to do. This exercise also builds strength and flexibility, and you may find that you're able to walk and stand longer without your feet starting to hurt. Suddenly, you'll get that youthful spring back in your step.

DON'TS

- ❑ **Do not stick out your buttocks or stomach.**
- ❑ **Do not allow your buttocks to drop lower than your knees.**
- ❑ **Do not let your heels drop to the floor.**
- ❑ **Do not tense your shoulders.**

Repetitions						
Day 17	Day 18	Day 19	Day 20	Day 21	Day 22	Days 23-30
5	5	5	5	5	5	5

Plié and Balance

TECHNIQUE

❑ Repeat as for Days 10-16, lifting your heels even higher so that you are balancing on the balls of your feet, heels together and your feet turned out even further. Lower your body 6 inches.

NOTE: As you get stronger, you may go down lower than six inches. Just be sure that you do not allow the buttocks to drop lower than your knees, or you will put tremendous pressure on your knees. Before long, you will have the feeling of 'floating' like a ballerina!

Repetitions						
Day 17	Day 18	Day 19	Day 20	Day 21	Day 22	Days 23-30
8	8	8	9	9	9	10

DON'TS

❑ **Do not stick out your buttocks or your stomach.**

❑ **Do not drop your heels, going down or coming up.**

❑ **Do not tense your shoulders.**

The Hamstring Stretch (Up and Over)

Technique

❑ Repeat as for Days 5-9, straightening your raised leg as much as you can! Your barre should now be at least hip high. This time, move your torso up, over, and down the length of your leg as far as you can, continuing to rest your hands on your lower leg.

❑ Work both sides.

NOTE: As your muscles stretch, you will be able to bend further and further over your leg. Some people eventually will be able to rest their heads on their legs. Again, if you are very flexible and you need more of a stretch, scoot the standing leg further back from the barre. You can also get more of a stretch by flexing the raised foot.

Repetitions TO EACH SIDE						
Day 17	Day 18	Day 19	Day 20	Day 21	Day 22	Days 23-30
40	40	45	45	45	45	50

DON'TS

❑ Do not lock either of your knees.

❑ Do not rest your hands on your knees.

❑ Do not make jerking movements with your neck or torso.

❑ Do not force the raised leg straight by pushing the leg or knee down with your hands.

❑ Do not force the raised leg higher than it can easily reach.

❑ Do not put your foot on something so high you cannot keep your balance.

❑ Do not tense your neck and shoulders.

The Hamstring and Calf Stretch

TECHNIQUE

❑ Repeat as for Days 10-16, continuing to work on straightening your raised leg as much as possible. Once you can do this, and only then, concentrate on sliding your extended foot forward until your extended leg is straight out on the floor. Hold for a count of 30 before beginning the repetitions.

❑ Work both sides.

NOTE: Once you can perform this exercise with your leg straight out on the floor, you will be stretching the front of the thighs and the difficult-to-reach ilio-psoas. (This is the group of muscles that attach to the front part of the vertebrae in your lower back, deep in the abdomen, and come forward to attach to your femur, or thigh bone. The ilio-psoas allows you to flex the thigh and also to flex the torso without moving your legs.)

Repetitions TO EACH SIDE

Day 17	Day 18	Day 19	Day 20	Day 21	Day 22	Days 23-30
40	40	40	45	45	45	50

DON'TS

- ❑ **Do not bounce.**
- ❑ **Do not force the raised leg forward by pulling it.**
- ❑ **Do not force the raised leg to straighten.**
- ❑ **Do not tense your neck.**

The Pelvic Rotation

TECHNIQUE

- ❑ Repeat as for Days 10-16.

NOTE: The stronger you get, the lower you will be able to keep your body and the more you will be able to circle with ease. Soon you will be lifting your body only a few inches off your heels.

You will be able to perform this movement smoothly and quickly, taking your hips even further out to the sides and curling up your pelvis even more. With this greater flexibility and range of motion, you will be able to do more repetitions with ease.

DON'TS

- ❑ **Do not arch your back.**
- ❑ **Do not stick out your stomach.**
- ❑ **Do not try to do too much too fast.**

Repetitions IN EACH DIRECTION

Day 17	Day 18	Day 19	Day 20	Day 21	Day 22	Days 23-30
5	5	5	5	5	5	5

The Pelvic Scoop

Technique

❏ Repeat as for Days 10-16, lowering your buttocks as if you were going to sit down until you feel them lightly touch your heels. Tighten your buttock muscles and slowly curl up your pelvis.

❏ Try to straighten your torso and aim your arms straight up; then return to your starting position, making sure you push your knees together, to make the leg muscles work even more.

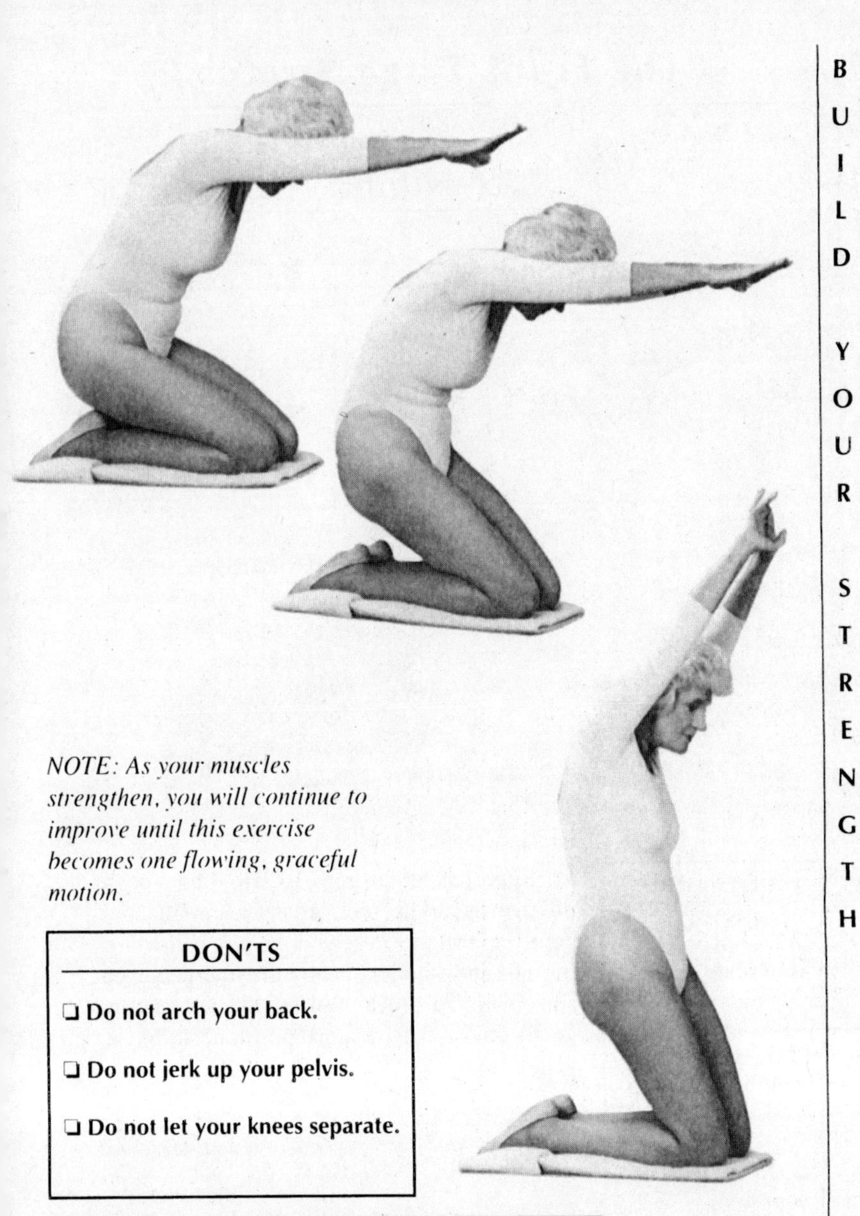

NOTE: As your muscles strengthen, you will continue to improve until this exercise becomes one flowing, graceful motion.

DON'TS

- ❑ Do not arch your back.
- ❑ Do not jerk up your pelvis.
- ❑ Do not let your knees separate.

Repetitions						
Day 17	Day 18	Day 19	Day 20	Day 21	Day 22	Days 23-30
5	5	5	5	5	5	5

The Front-Thigh Stretch

TECHNIQUE

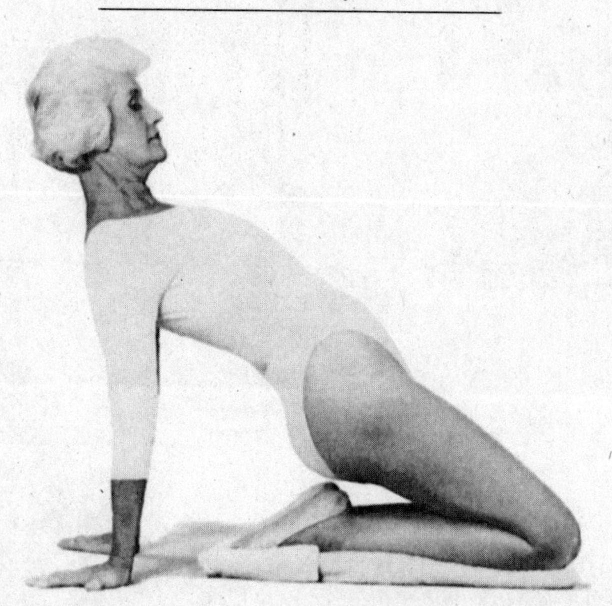

DON'TS

- ❑ **Do not arch your back or stick out your stomach.**
- ❑ **Do not allow your head to drop back.**
- ❑ **Do not tense your body.**
- ❑ **Do not hunch your shoulders or tense your neck.**

❑ Repeat as for Days 10-16. Hold for a count of 10, then curl up your pelvis even more than before and slowly raise your body ½ inch more. In triple slow motion, gently lift your pelvis up and down ¼ to ½ inch. Release the buttocks and gently return to the original position, sitting on your heels.

NOTE: As you become stronger, you will be able to curl up your pelvis even more, while relaxing your entire body completely.

Repetitions

Day 17	Day 18	Day 19	Day 20	Day 21	Day 22	Days 23-30
10	10	10	10	10	10	10

The Inner-Thigh Squeeze

Technique

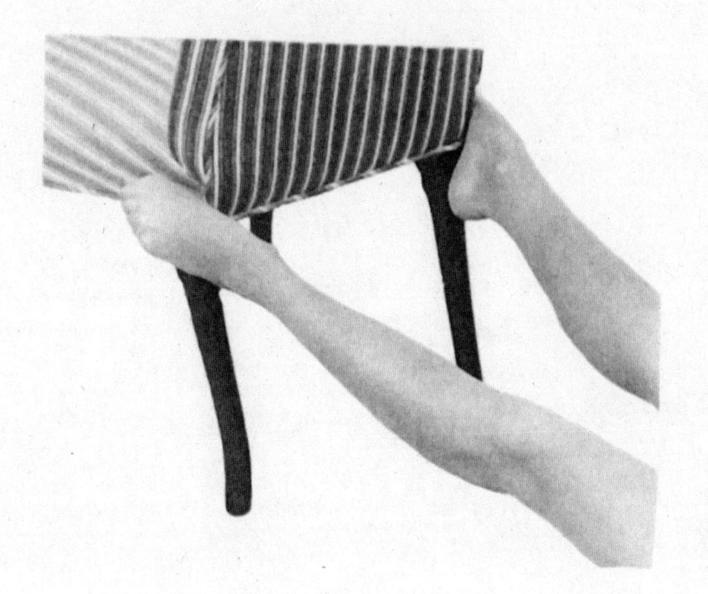

❑ Repeat as for Days 10-16, continuing to raise your legs 1 to 2 inches at a time, until you have reached a maximum of 6 to 8 inches off the floor.

DON'TS

❑ **Do not squeeze and release; hold steadily for the count.**

❑ **Do not tense your shoulders.**

❑ **Do not lock your knees.**

Repetitions						
Day 17	Day 18	Day 19	Day 20	Day 21	Day 22	Days 23-30
75	75	75	100	100	100	100